Game for All Seasons
Cookbook

Dedication

To Dana for reminding me.
And to Amy, Ann Marie, Bridget, Casey, Chris, David, Edwin, Evan,
Jeffrey, James, Marie, Miranda, Petra, Tabitha, Tiffany, Robert,
Stephanie, Susan, and J. for encouraging me.

Game for All Seasons
Cookbook

Harold Webster

Great American Publishers

www.greatamericanpublishers.com

• TOLL-FREE **866.625.9241**•

Recipe Collection © 2007 by Harold Webster

Great American Publishers

P. O. Box 1305 • Kosciusko, MS 39090
TOLL-FREE 866.625.9241 • www.greatamericanpublishers.com

ISBN 978-0-9779053-1-7

Printed in Canada

FIRST EDITON
10 9 8 7 6 5 4 3 2 1

Written by Harold Webster
Cover design • Mark Anderson • Big Whiskey Design Studio
Inside layout and design • Sheila Simmons
Front cover photo and food styling • Harold Webster
Back cover photo • Dana Fennell

Game for All Seasons Cookbook
• Table of Contents •

Summer, CONTINUED

Fall

Fall, CONTINUED

Winter

Author's Remarks

photo by: Anne Webster

These stories of my life were not initially intended to be written and published as monograph. They were originally published as individual weekly newspaper columns during a two year period of time between my retirement from the world of daily toil and the time that I became weary of being retired and my lifelong dream of working towards an advanced degree in archaeology. These weekly columns provided me with the occasion and the time to reflect upon my years and to place these years and memories into perspective and onto paper before they vanished.

This is a fine cookbook and one that contains even finer recipes. However, this is more than just a first-rate game, fish, and fowl cookbook. It is the chronicle of a young boy and his journey through the phases of his life. If one were to say that this work is an autobiography about a romantic, 20th century hunter-gatherer, I would not disagree.

It is a story about the transit of time and the end of an era when the tempo of life was less hurried and when one had the comfort of place and the time to pause and to witness and the moment to ponder upon what is true in the heart.

When I reflect back on the previous sixty-four years of my life, I question where the years have gone. Did I misuse years in my youth that I could have applied to more lucrative endeavors? Some may answer yes. However, I will argue that what I have observed, what I have experienced, and what I lived through in my life, money cannot buy, because I have the memories and they give me a deep sense of personal fulfillment and satisfaction that nourishes me as I look forward to my remaining years and a life that is about turning the things that I want to do into things that I have done.

Harold Webster
Pinehaven/University of Southern Mississippi

Introduction

A good friend has a theory about hunting and fishing, one that he tries to live by. "No matter how busy you are, no matter what you do for a living, make a point of taking at least one special hunting or fishing trip every year," he says. "Do that and before you know it you'll have built up a lifetime of fine memories."

That's solid advice, and I've lived by it as much as possible. Like Harold Webster, I've had the good fortune to have hunted and fished across the country, and in many parts of the world. Along the way, I've met fine people, experienced wild, beautiful, and varied terrain, and taken a fair share of fish and game. I've stockpiled memories of my own, and I always look forward to planning my next trip.

My most recent one was near Onward, Mississippi, near the Little Sunflower River, where President Theodore Roosevelt hunted for bear in 1902. That's when he refused to shoot a tethered black bear, hence spawning the name "Teddy Bear."

On this hunt, I was with friend and outfitter Alton Norris from Cary, Mississippi. Alton, his buddies, and I saddled up our horses on New Year's morning, unleashed a pack of hounds into the thick woods of the Delta, and went riding after them. Unbelievably, by 11:00 a.m. we had managed to find and take a 250-pound wild boar, one with a thick hide and razor-sharp tusks. After the inevitable handshaking all around, plus a serious moment of reverence for this fallen wild game animal, we all piled into the trucks and headed back to Alton's for a grand feast. Another memory was in my book.

That hog is currently in my freezer at home in New York. Now the good part begins: deciding on different recipes, inviting friends and family over for great dinners, and recounting the story of my hunt with colleagues from the South.

Author Harold Webster lives near Jackson, Mississippi, and knows Southern cuisine as well as anyone alive. When I told him about my wild boar hunt, how we had all gone back to Alton's place for a huge meal after the hunt, and what a pleasure it had been for this Yankee to spend time with his Southern friends, he agreed that hunters all have a common bond, no matter where they come from. He also said that the camaraderie I found there was typical.

"That's the nature of the South," he said. "It's part of our culture to invite people into our homes and treat them as part of the family. Food is a big part of it. Good food and being social go hand and hand."

That is one of the reasons Harold got into cooking in the first place. When he was a boy, he used to watch his mother cook, watch her prepare grand meals for friends and family. ("Her chocolate éclairs were my favorite," Harold will tell you with a wink.) One thing lead to another, and now Harold has become one of the finest game chefs you'll ever know. He's written three cookbooks (this one, *Game for All Seasons*, *The Complete Venison Cookbook*, and *The Venison Sausage Cookbook*). He has won international cooking awards, he has dined and taught cooking across the world, he's written for magazines, appeared on national TV and radio shows, and he's given food seminars at sportsmen's shows and at universities.

Through it all, good food, fine dining, and the comradeship that goes with it have been his guiding lights. In this book, you'll get a glimpse into what makes Harold tick, into the events that shaped his life. Each recipe in this remarkable book is accompanied by a vignette about the game being prepared and cooked. In these, Harold regales you with tales of squirrel hunting when he was a boy with his Feist dog, Poochie; or listening to his grandfather tell him about cooking chili in Texas during World War II; or fishing for king mackerel off a Gulf Coast oil rig when he got out of college; or cooking up mule deer steaks at a hunting lodge in Nevada.

Some have called Harold a "romantic, 20th Century hunter-gatherer," and I think that's on the mark. Every recipe is prefaced with a tale from his heart; together they make up a lifetime's worth of memories, not to mention some very fine eating.

So enjoy. And now, if you'll excuse me, there's a Cajun Roasted Wild Hog recipe on page 137 that I'm putting together right now. The kids are home from college for mid-winter break, some friends are due to arrive in a few hours, and I've got to get busy.

Jay Cassell, Deputy Editor
Field & Stream magazine

Spring

Mud, Bugs, and Crawfish Tails

It was Bobby LeBlanc's dad that taught me how to cook crawfish. I spent several years of my misspent youth working in the Louisiana oil fields. Being off every other week gave me a great deal of time to meet and enjoy the local populace. One Saturday in April, Mr. LaBlanc invited me to go with him to his favorite crawfish "hole" and catch a mess for dinner. Well, it wasn't a "hole" it was a 20-acre area filled with 6-inch-deep black water. We baited two-dozen crawfish traps with chicken livers and set them out in a large circle. We waited 15 or so minutes and then began walking around the circle and gently lifting each net. My first surprise was that in each net we had two to four crawfish. In short order, we had a 5-gallon bucket full of the clicking creatures. That was a lot easier than netting saltwater crabs. After boiling our catch, Mr. LaBlanc sat me on a wooden bench at the kitchen table and told me to start shucking. My second surprise was that after shucking the whole 5-gallons, I only had three quarts of tails for all my labor. I still go crawdad fishing every year or so, but I much prefer to fish for crawdads at the grocery store.

Fried Crawfish Tails

Cooking oil
1 pound peeled crawfish tails or shrimp
Salt and cayenne pepper
1 egg, lightly beaten
Dash white vinegar
¼ cup water
1 teaspoon baking powder
¼ cup flour
¼ cup Italian-style breadcrumbs

Heat 4-inches of oil in a deep pot or electric fryer. Season crawfish tails with salt and pepper. Mix egg, vinegar, water, and baking powder; add tails. Combine flour and breadcrumbs and toss the tails to coat. Fry a few at a time and drain. Serves 4.

Crawfish Patties

1 pound crawfish tails
1 onion, finely chopped
4 garlic cloves, minced
¼ cup minced parsley
6 green onions, finely chopped
1 cup plain breadcrumbs
1 to 2 tablespoons Creole seasoning or to taste
4 eggs lightly beaten, divided
1 tablespoon Worcestershire sauce
¼ to ½ teaspoon Tabasco sauce (optional)
Salt and pepper
Cornmeal

Grind the tails together with the next four ingredients. Mix in breadcrumbs, creole seasoning, two of the beaten eggs, Worcestershire sauce, Tabasco sauce, salt and pepper. Shape into patties and dip into remaining eggs, roll in cornmeal and fry until golden brown. Serves 4.

Crawfish Cornbread

4 eggs, beaten
4 cups yellow cornmeal
6 teaspoons baking powder
2 teaspoons salt
4 cups cream-style corn
2 cups whole milk
8 tablespoons butter, melted
4 teaspoons sugar
½ pound shredded Cheddar cheese
1 pound crawfish tails

Mix all ingredients together and bake at 375° for about 1 hour or until the top is brown and sounds hollow when tapped. Serve as an appetizer or topped with crawfish étouffée or serve topped with grilled fish. Serves 6 to 8.

Crawfish Stew

½ cup butter
5 tablespoons flour
2 large onions, minced
1 green pepper, minced
2 ribs celery, finely chopped
1 (16-ounce) can tomato sauce
2 pounds cooked crawfish tails
¼ teaspoon cayenne pepper (optional)
Cooked rice for 4 to 6

Melt butter in a large skillet, add flour and stir over low heat until golden brown. Add onions, green pepper, and celery; cook until just soft. Add tomato sauce and crawfish. If very thick add water. Cover and simmer 30 minutes. Scrape bottom often. Serve hot with cooked rice on the side. Serves 4 to 6.

Wing Shooting at the Grocery Store

The older I get, the worse my eyes get, and the worse wing shot I am. For us older folks, quail hunting may be a thing of the past. There are not as many quail as there used to be and some people say it is because of changes in our agricultural patterns. Last fall I was walking through my local grocery store and out of curiosity I looked into the upright freezer section and found boxes of individually packaged quail, priced at $1.40 per quail. They come packed 12 per box and since I eat two to three per sitting, I loaded up with four boxes. My niece, J., who is also my hunting and eating buddy, has never eaten quail and I am hoping that later in the spring she and I can reach into the freezer and do a little "Wing Shooting" and cooking together.

Fried Quail with Onion Gravy

16 quail
Salt and pepper
Flour
4 slices bacon
1 cup cooking oil
3 tablespoons flour
½ to ¾ cup milk
⅓ onion, minced
Garlic powder

Sprinkle quail with salt and pepper; dredge in flour and set aside. Fry bacon and save for other uses. Add cooking oil to bacon drippings and heat. Add quail and cook 10 to 12 minutes on each side or until done. Remove quail and drain. Stir 3 tablespoons flour to milk and gradually whisk into oil. Add onion and cook over medium heat until thickened. Stir in ¼ teaspoon salt, a sprinkling of pepper and a dash of garlic powder. Serves 4 to 6.

Quail in Sour Cream Sauce

8 quail
Salt and pepper
Garlic powder
Flour
2 sticks butter
1 pint sour cream

Preheat oven to 350°. Season quail with salt, pepper and garlic powder; dust with flour. Melt butter and fry quail over medium heat until lightly browned. Pour 3 tablespoons butter into a baking dish and add a single layer of quail, breast-up. Lightly sprinkle with flour. Cover with sour cream and bake 35 minutes. Serves 4.

Baked Quail with Mushrooms

⅓ cup flour
1 teaspoon salt
½ teaspoon pepper
6 quail
2 tablespoons plus ½ cup butter, divided
½ pound mushrooms, sliced
¼ cup plus 1 tablespoon flour
2 cups chicken broth
½ cup sherry or water
6 cups cooked rice

Preheat oven to 350°. Combine ¼ cup flour, salt and pepper; dredge quail and set aside. Melt 2 tablespoons butter in a skillet, add mushrooms and sauté 4 minutes. Remove and set aside. Melt ½ cup butter and brown quail on both sides. Remove quail and place in a casserole dish. Add remaining 1 tablespoon flour to skillet and drippings and stir for one minute. Gradually add broth and sherry or water and cook over medium heat, stirring constantly until thickened. Stir in saved mushrooms. Pour gravy over quail and bake 1 hour. Serves 4.

There's Nothing my Skillet won't Fry

The traditional way of cooking anything is to fry it. There are very few types of game or fish that are not able to be fried. I grew up with a 5-gallon lard bucket sitting in the corner of my grandmother's kitchen. It was used for everything from making biscuits to soothing wasp stings. We did not have all the health problems that are associated with saturated fat that we have today. My feeling is that we were healthy because we ate a balanced diet that was high in vegetables and fresh fruits and very low in sugar and processed foods. Lard is a thing of the past and oils low in fat and cholesterol are the current standard. Now and then I just have to indulge myself in a good, old dinner fried in lard. As I very seldom eat fast food, I don't think that frying in lard once every 6 months or so will shorten my life more than a day or so. For the remainder of the time, I use frying and cooking oils that are labeled as "low" or "no."

Creole-Style Crab Cakes

1 pound crabmeat
4 slices bread, trimmed and torn into 2-inch pieces
½ cup olive oil
2 large eggs, lightly beaten
1 teaspoon mustard powder
½ teaspoon each salt and white pepper
2 teaspoons Worcestershire sauce
2 tablespoons mayonnaise
2 tablespoons minced fresh parsley
2 teaspoons lemon juice
1 cup cracker meal
Cooking oil

Combine all ingredients except cracker meal and oil. Shape into cakes 4-inches long x 3-inches wide x 1¼-inches thick. Roll in cracker meal and press gently. Fry 2 cakes at a time until golden brown. Serves 4.

Fried Frog Legs

1 cup white wine, white grape juice or water
½ each teaspoon salt and pepper
1 teaspoon chopped parsley
½ small onion, sliced
Dash ground nutmeg
16 pair frog legs
2 eggs, lightly beaten
1 cup flour
1 cup cooking oil

Combine wine, salt, pepper, parsley, onion, and nutmeg; cover frog legs with mixture and marinate 1 hour. Remove legs, dip in egg and roll in flour. Fry in oil until brown. Serves 4.

Fried Venison Finger Steaks

1 pound venison steak, ½-inch strips
1 teaspoon lemon pepper seasoning
½ teaspoon salt
½ cup buttermilk
1 egg, beaten
1 cup flour
¾ cup shortening or cooking oil

Pound venison to ½-inch thickness. Sprinkle with lemon pepper and season with salt. Cut steaks into ½-inch strips. Mix buttermilk and egg. Dip strips into mixture and roll in flour. Preheat a skillet; add oil and brown steaks on both sides. Do not over-cook. Serves 3 to 4.

Fried Whole Small Bass

2 large eggs
2 tablespoons cold water
1½ cups flour
1¼ teaspoons salt
¼ teaspoon pepper
Scant ⅛ teaspoon red pepper (optional)
4 (1- to 2-pound) bass
¼ cup salted butter
¼ cup olive oil
⅓ cup minced green onions
1 bay leaf, crumbled
¾ teaspoon dried marjoram

Whisk together eggs and water. Mix together flour, salt and peppers, and set aside. Coat fish with egg, roll in flour mixture, and set aside 5 minutes. Melt butter in a skillet; add olive oil and fry fish until beginning to brown. Add green onions, bay leaf, and marjoram. Turn fish and brown on other side; remove and allow to drain. Simmer the sauce 3 minutes to reduce and spoon over bass. Serves 4.

Young Harold with the whole bass.

It's Oyster Shucking Time

Contrary to the "Old Husbands Tale" oysters are good to eat twelve months of the year. The story about oysters being good only in the "R" months is because before refrigerated trucks, the "R" months were the coldest months of the year and shipping fresh seafood during these months prevented spoilage. My favorite oyster recipe is actually a non-recipe. I like them raw and a lot of them—with lemon and a little horseradish and a touch of Tabasco sauce in the ketchup. As a young lad, I was introduced to eating them raw in Felix's Oyster House by my dad and have liked them that way ever since. My dad would lift me to the counter and tell the shucker to keep shucking until I was full. Oysters are one of the more versatile of shellfish. Oysters can be eaten raw, baked in the shell with a cream sauce, made into a wonderful soup, grilled, fried, sautéed, stewed, and gumbo-ed. Any way that you like to cook, you can find a recipe for oysters; and all of them are good.

How To Shuck Oysters:
Make sure oysters are still alive by checking that their shells are tightly closed. To save the liquid, work over a bowl and hold oyster in the palm of your hand with a towel. Or, lay oyster on a folded kitchen towel and hold steady with one hand. Position the oyster with the cup-side down so the flatter side faces up. Insert a dull paring or oyster knife between the shells, near the hinge. Twist the knife so that the oysters' muscles are detached. Lift the top shell and cut the muscle attaching the meat into the bottom shell.

Oyster Stir Fry

1 tablespoon cornstarch
1 tablespoon water
1½ tablespoons cooking oil
1 garlic clove, minced
2 tablespoons chopped green onion
1 tablespoon peeled and minced fresh ginger
¾ pound raw oysters
⅓ cup orange juice
2 tablespoons soy sauce
Cooked rice for 4

Mix cornstarch with water and set aside. Heat oil in a skillet or wok; add garlic, onion, and ginger and stir-fry 1 minute. Add oysters, orange juice, soy sauce, and cornstarch mixture; cook until sauce begins to thicken. Serve immediately over rice. Serves 4.

Oyster and Venison Sausage Turnover Appetizer

1 pound venison breakfast or other sausage
1 cup minced onion
1 pint raw oysters, drained
⅓ cup grated sharp Cheddar cheese
⅓ cup grated mozzarella cheese
1 package puff pastry, cut into 16 squares
Butter

Preheat oven to 425°. Sauté sausage and onions; stirring to break up sausage. Add oysters, stir once, and remove immediately; drain. Discard fat. Place oyster/sausage mixture in a bowl and mix in cheeses. Place the puff pastry squares on buttered baking sheets and spoon the oyster/sausage mixture onto the center of the pastry. Fold pastry over and crimp edges with a fork. Bake 10 minutes or until golden and crisp. Makes 16.

Curried Oyster Casserole

2 cups cooked wild rice
½ cup butter, melted
4 dozen raw oysters
Salt and pepper
1 can cream of chicken soup
1 cup cream
1½ tablespoons onion powder
¾ teaspoon thyme
1 tablespoon curry powder
¼ cup hot water

Preheat oven to 300°. Combine cooked wild rice with butter. Place half the rice in a casserole dish; add half of the oysters. Season with salt and pepper to taste; repeat layers. Combine remaining ingredients in a saucepan and warm. Pour over oysters and bake 45 minutes. Serves 4.

Young as a Spring Turkey

When the dogwoods bloom, the turkeys are out. Spring turkey hunting is a right of passage for the young at heart. I only came to appreciate the wild turkey in the second half of my life. While growing up, there just were no turkeys in my area and very few turkeys anywhere else either. Today, six months don't go by without me seeing a turkey or two crossing the dirt road leading to our home. Three falls ago, I had a flock of six hens that walked through my yard every afternoon and drank from my pond. That was until my neighbor decided to bulldoze his forest and turn the cover into bush-hogged pastureland. Well, I own that land now and it is re-planted in mixed hardwoods and pines. Last week I heard a turkey gobble. Geese and duck can be unpredictably tough and stringy but not wild turkey. I bought myself one of those turkey deep fryers and am waiting on the opportunity to first practice on the grocery story variety in preparation for J., Will, and I trying it out on our native variety.

Smoked Wild Turkey

½ cup olive oil
1½ tablespoons rosemary
1½ tablespoons thyme leaves
3 garlic cloves, minced
1 clean wild turkey
4 celery stalks, quartered
5 onions, quartered, divided
Natural toothpicks
1 pound thick-sliced smoked bacon
Hickory chips soaked in water

Whisk together oil, rosemary, thyme, and garlic; rub turkey inside and out with mixture. Stuff turkey with celery and 3 onions. Separate remaining 2 onions and secure over turkey with white toothpicks. Cover with bacon strips. Place turkey in smoker and smoke 6 to 8 hours. Replenish hickory chips as needed. Serves 6 to 8.

Baked Wild Turkey

1 wild turkey
Garlic powder, salt and black pepper
Roasting bag
4 stalks celery, quartered
2 carrots, quartered
3 medium onions, sliced thick
4 bacon strips
1 stick butter, melted

Sprinkle turkey with garlic powder, salt, and pepper. Place turkey in a roasting bag and place vegetables along side. Lay bacon strips on top and cover with melted butter. Close bag, make a small hole in bag and insert a meat thermometer into thickest part; bake at 325° for 2 to 3 hours until meat thermometer reads 180°. Serves 6 to 8.

Fried Wild Turkey Breast

1 wild turkey breast
1 egg
1 cup cream
1 cup flour
Lemon pepper and salt
Cooking oil

Slice turkey breast across the grain into finger-sized pieces. Lightly beat egg and cream; and turkey pieces to coat. Mix flour and lemon pepper and salt to taste; roll pieces in flour. Fry in oil until just brown. Do not over-cook. Serves 4.

Turkey and Wild Rice Casserole

2 cups wild rice
1 cup brown rice
5 cups chicken broth
1 pound mushrooms, sliced
4 cups diced cooked wild turkey
2 cans chicken broth
4 tablespoons chopped onion
½ teaspoon chopped garlic
Salt and pepper
1 pint cream
1 teaspoon butter
2 cups chopped celery
1 can water chestnuts, sliced
4 tablespoons Parmesan cheese

Preheat oven to 350°. Combine wild rice and brown rice with chicken broth; cook until done. Toss cooked rice, mushrooms and turkey. Add remaining ingredients except cheese. Pour into a baking dish and sprinkle with cheese. Bake 1 hour. Serves 4 to 6.

Float Fishing for Smallmouth Bass

It does not require fancy equipment to take a couple of young nieces and nephews
float fishing. All you need is: young ones, a flat-bottom boat, cane poles, a paddle or
two, life preservers, and a slow-moving stream. Smallmouth bass are indigenous to
small creeks and streams, and like trout, they face upstream in hopes of catching a
bug or a worm floating by or a crawfish caught in the current. Toss your lines down-
stream of the boat and let the current carry both the cork and the boat along. Paddle
only enough to steer the boat without making it go faster than the current. Inquire
about float times at the local Gas-Gro and Bait store. This would also be a
good time to pick up a loaf of light bread, slices of hoop cheese, bologna,
mayonnaise, and cream sodas for an elegant lunch on a sand bar. The kids
will always remember this fishing trip as being the best and the one with
the finest food.

Broiled Smallmouth Bass

4 (8-ounce) bass fillets
¼ cup butter, melted
1 tablespoon lemon pepper
½ teaspoon red pepper (optional)
1 large onion, sliced thin and separated
2 teaspoons Worcestershire sauce
2 lemons

Preheat oven to 450°. Dip fillets into melted butter and place in a broiler
pan. Sprinkle with lemon pepper and red pepper. Place onion rings on
bass; drizzle on Worcestershire sauce. Bake 8 minutes. Turn broiler up to
500° to brown fish and onions about 3 to 6 minutes. Squeeze lemons on top.
Serves 2 to 4.

Beer Battered Smallmouth Bass

4 smallmouth bass
Lemon juice
6 tablespoons flour
2 tablespoons yellow cornmeal
½ teaspoon dill
1 teaspoon salt
½ teaspoon tarragon
1 tablespoon paprika
¼ (3-ounce) can beer
1 tablespoon cooking oil or lard

Sprinkle bass inside and out with lemon juice. Mix flour, cornmeal, dill, salt, tarragon and paprika in a bowl. Stir in beer and beat until smooth. Dip bass into the batter one at a time and sauté in the cooking oil or lard until firm, approximately 8 to 9 minutes per side. Serves 3 to 4.

Bass-Almond Sauté

1 cup milk
1 egg, lightly beaten
1 cup flour
½ teaspoon salt
2 pounds smallmouth bass fillets
½ cup cooking oil or lard
1½ cups sliced mushrooms
½ cup chopped smoked almonds
3 tablespoons butter
2 tablespoons chopped parsley
1 tablespoon lemon juice

Combine milk and egg. In a separate bowl, mix four and salt. Dip fillets into egg mixture and then coat in flour mixture. Sauté fish in oil over medium heat. Combine remaining ingredients in saucepan and sauté over medium heat 5 to 7 minutes. Transfer fish to individual dishes and cover with mushroom/almond sauce. Serves 4 to 6.

Brownies in Lemon-Apple Sauce

¾ cup apple juice
Grated peel and juice of ½ lemon
½ pound smallmouth bass fillets
¼ teaspoon dry dill weed
½ tablespoon apple butter
½ tablespoon honey
½ tablespoon Dijon mustard
1 tablespoon cornstarch
1 cup cooked rice
2 tablespoons sliced green onion

In a large skillet, combine apple juice and lemon peel and juice. Add bass and sprinkle with dill. Bring to a boil, reduce heat, cover and simmer 10 to 12 minutes or until flesh is just firm. Remove fish. To the skillet add apple butter, honey, mustard and cornstarch. Stir until melted. Serve fish with cooked rice, spoon over sauce and sprinkle with green onion. Serves 2.

Key Lime & Lemon Sorbet

1¼ cups sugar
1¼ cups water
1 cup lemon juice
¾ cup key lime juice

Mix sugar and water in a saucepan; bring to boil and set aside to cool. Stir in lemon and lime juice; process in an ice cream machine. Serve in chilled wine glasses. Serves 8 to 10.

Cobia: It Ain't no Lemon

The cobia is a powerful fish and a thrilling catch. Once the fish is hooked, the thrill usually begins by lots of line coming screaming off the reel and the inability of the angler to do anything but hang on. Besides cobia, this species of fish goes under many names — the most common are lemon fish, ling, and sergeant fish. Cobia can be found in all tropical waters. They migrate to the south in winter and as far north as the Carolinas in summer — in water that ranges between 68 and 86 degrees. Although cobia can weight as much as 170 pounds normal catches are more in the 30- to 40-pound range. It is the size of the fish and the firmness of the meat that makes cobia so versatile in the kitchen. Large steaks and fillets lend themselves to grilling and broiling. Fresh cobia is available year-round in most grocery stores, however don't buy fish that has been frozen and then defrosted for more than two days. If your store is out of cobia, any firm-fleshed saltwater fish will substitute in these recipes.

Young Harold with his
large cobia.

Poached Fillets of Cobia

2 (½-inch thick) cobia fillets
Juice of 3 lemons, divided
1 bay leaf, crumbled
Salt and pepper
Toothpicks
½ pound butter
1 tablespoon flour
½ cup dry white wine (optional)
Lemon juice
½ pint cream
2 egg yolks, well beaten

Marinate fillets in juice of two lemons and bay leaf in refrigerator for 1 hour. Sprinkle with salt and pepper. Roll and secure with a toothpick. Place in a deep pan, cover with water, cover pot and poach for 5 minutes. Strain water and reserve. Melt butter, stir in flour, and simmer until golden. Add strained fish stock and boil to reduce for 15 minutes. Strain and season to taste with wine and lemon juice. Keep sauce hot; mix cream and egg yolks and stir into sauce. Remove toothpicks from fish and cover with sauce. Serves 2.

Marinated and Grilled Cobia

3 pounds cobia fillets or steaks
⅓ cup olive oil
⅓ cup lemon juice
1½ teaspoons powdered mustard
1 garlic clove, minced
1 teaspoon salt
¼ teaspoon pepper

Mix all ingredients and marinate cobia in refrigerator for 15 minutes. Grill on both sides until flesh just firms. Baste with marinade. Serves 4 to 6.

Grilled Cobia with Tropical Fruit Medley

½ cup butter plus additional to taste
4 cups mixed, pineapple, kiwi, mango, papaya, and other fruits
1 cup fresh orange juice
¼ cup grated coconut
4 cobia fillets, cut to serving size
Lemon
1 cup slivered almonds

Melt butter in saucepan. Add fruit, juice and coconut; heat gently until flavors are mixed. Place cobia servings on a piece of aluminum foil, season with lemon and butter to taste. Cover with fruit mixture and garnish with almond slivers. Cook on the grill 10 to 15 minutes or until flesh is firm. Do not turn. Serves 4.

Broiled Cobia with Breaded Eggplant

2 servings Cobia, finger-size
½ cup lemon juice
Salt and pepper
½ cup olive oil
1 eggplant, ¼-inch slices
1 cup flour
1 egg, slightly beaten
1 cup Italian seasoned breadcrumbs
¼ pound butter, sliced

Marinate cobia in lemon juice, salt and pepper for 10 minutes. Brush with olive oil and broil until just firm. Dip eggplant slices into flour, then egg, then breadcrumbs. Place sliced butter and eggplant on a tray and bake 25 minutes at 400°. Place cobia on eggplant and serve. Serves 2.

Where you find Shellfish:
You will find Pompano

Pompano are schooling fish and where you see one, there are probably more. Pompano love sand fleas, small crabs, and other small shellfish. Bridge pilings are a great place to fish because of the years of barnacle build up and an abundance of small crabs, shrimp, and other creatures living amongst the barnacles. When fishing around pilings, take a shovel or hoe and scrape the barnacles off the pilings to create a chum. You'll be surprised at what you will attract. Light tackle with 6- to 8-pound line works best because pompano have no teeth and with their keen eyesight may see heavier line. Pompano are always moving, so fish them on the bottom with a weight small enough to hold the bait down, but not so big as to hinder its movement along the bottom. If you find a spot of beach with a lot of sand fleas, then you know that is a good spot for pompano. Pompano are available in the seafood sections of many grocery stores.

Miss Anne bridge
fishing for pompano.

Pompano Amandine

6 pompano fillets
½ teaspoon salt
¼ teaspoon pepper
¼ cup flour
12 tablespoons butter, divided
2 tablespoons cooking oil
2 tablespoons lemon juice
2 tablespoons chopped parsley
1 cup sliced and toasted almonds
6 lemon slices

Skin fillets and wash with cold water. Dry, season with salt and pepper and dredge in flour. Heat 4 tablespoons butter and 2 tablespoons oil in a skillet. Cook fillets on both sides until brown and flesh is just firm. Remove to a platter. Melt remaining butter until brown and pour, along with lemon juice, over fish. Sprinkle with parsley and toasted almonds. Serve with lemon slices. Serves 6.

Pompano with Egg Dressing

2 hard-boiled eggs
French dressing
4 pompano fillets
Salt and pepper
Flour
3 tablespoons butter

Chop hard-boiled eggs and add just enough French dressing to hold together. Season pompano with salt and pepper and dredge in flour. Sauté fillets in butter about 8 minutes. When done, spoon egg dressing onto each serving. Serves 4.

Scaloppini of Pompano

1 cup chopped onion
½ cup canola oil, divided
1½ pounds chopped tomatoes
2 garlic cloves, minced
1 cup tomato juice
Salt and pepper
2 pounds pompano fillets
1 tablespoon lemon juice
½ cup flour
8 ounces egg noodles
Fresh parsley, minced

Sauté onion in half the oil until tender. Add chopped tomatoes, garlic, tomato juice, and salt and pepper to taste. Cook 15 minutes over low heat. Flatten pompano fillets with a mallet, season with salt, pepper and lemon juice. Dredge in flour and sauté briskly in remaining oil. Cook noodles in salted water, drain and arrange on serving platter. Top with pompano and cover with hot tomato and onion sauce. Sprinkle with parsley. Serves 6.

Baked Oyster-Pompano

4 pompano fillets
24 raw oysters
4 tablespoons butter
¼ cup water
Salt and pepper

Preheat oven to 300°. Place pompano fillets in a buttered baking pan. Top each fillet with 6 oysters and 1 tablespoon butter. Pour water into baking pan and bake 10 minutes or until flesh is firm. Season with salt and pepper. Serves 4.

The Specks are Running Wild

Speckled trout range from Texas up the Atlantic coast and can be caught year around. They are unusual in that respect; there are two distinct groups of anglers that fish for them. Winter fishermen and spring-summer fishermen. Some people wait until the cooler weather of the fall before venturing out in search of specks and reds in the coastal marshes. Others can't wait until spring-summer so they can hit the beaches, shallow water oil platforms, and larger bays in search of their quarry. These two groups are actually targeting two different groups of fish. The spring-summer fishermen that fish the surf and shallow rigs are fishing the adult population and therefore catch specks that are on the average much larger. Speckled trout usually begin their spawning runs in May and this is when they move to the beaches and passes where the actual spawning occurs.

Macadamia-Crusted Trout

6 tablespoons butter, divided
1 cup crushed macadamia nuts
4 teaspoons flour, divided
4 speckled trout fillets
1 cup milk
White and red pepper (optional)

Melt 4 tablespoons butter in skillet. Mix ground nuts and 2 teaspoons flour. Dip fillets in butter, then in nut/flour mixture and sauté about 4 minutes on both sides. Remove fish to a baking dish. Scrape bottom of skillet, melt 2 teaspoons butter, add 2 teaspoons flour, whisk in milk and peppers to make a thin sauce. Spoon sauce over fish and bake 15 minutes uncovered at 350°. Serves 2 to 4.

Poached Speckled Trout
with Herbed Mushroom Sauce

4 speckled trout, filleted
Fish or chicken stock
4 tablespoons butter
2 tablespoons chopped parsley
4 tablespoons chopped mushrooms
2 tablespoons chopped green onions
2 pieces stale white bread
Salt and pepper

Simmer trout in stock 15 to 18 minutes or until flesh is firm. In a skillet, melt butter and lightly sauté parsley, mushrooms, and onions; set aside. Soak stale bread in fish stock, squeeze out excess. Measure ¼ cup stock and stir, along with soaked bread, into vegetables. Season to taste. Lay fish on a platter and cover with herb mixture. Serves 4 to 6.

Stuffed Speckled Trout

¾ cup chopped onion, divided
¾ cup chopped celery, divided
1 cup butter, divided
1 pound crabmeat
1 pound shrimp, peeled
¾ cup breadcrumbs
Salt and red pepper
16 speckled trout fillets
2 garlic cloves, minced
¼ pound mushrooms, sliced
¼ cup white wine or water

Sauté ½ cup onions and ½ cup celery in ¼ cup butter. Add crabmeat and ¼ shrimp; simmer uncovered until shrimp begins to firm. Add breadcrumbs to thicken mixture; salt and pepper to taste. Set stuffing aside. Preheat oven to 350°. Butter two 9x13-inch baking dishes and place 4 fillets in each dish and top each with a scoop of stuffing and lay another fillet on top, cover with ¼ cup melted butter and bake 30 to 40 minutes or until flesh is firm. Make sauce by melting ½ cup butter and sautéing ¼ cup celery, ¼ cup onions, and garlic. Add ¾ shrimp and simmer until pink. Add mushrooms and white wine and simmer 3 to 5 minutes. Arrange trout on a serving plate and cover with sauce. Serves 8.

May is for Bream, Crickets, and Children

Bream always bite better on a full moon. The week before and after the full moon of May is the peak bream-bedding period of the year. The full moon of June is almost as good. Crickets are the bait of choice and it is not uncommon to catch fifty or more large bream in one bed. Gather up the family and take them to the shallow end of the nearest pond. Carry a pole for everybody but yourself, because you will not be doing any fishing. Your job will be to bait hooks, untangle lines, and stringer fish. If you don't have children, offer to take the neighbors and their children fishing. Children tire easily when the fish are not biting so do not miss this opportunity.

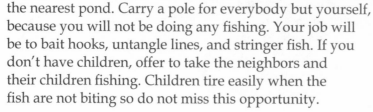

A young Harold waiting
for the next fishing trip.

Oven Baked Bream

I recommend baking bream for small children because you can easily remove all bones before serving.

12 cleaned bream
Olive oil
1 tablespoon chopped garlic
Salt and pepper
3 tablespoons chopped parsley

Preheat oven to 350°. Coat the fish inside and out with olive oil, rub with garlic, sprinkle with salt and pepper. Fill two baking pans with ¼-inch water and lay fish on bottom. Bake 20 minutes or until the fins pull loose. Gently pull loose the fins and lift off the top fillet. Turn the fish over and lift off the other fillet. Check for needle rib bones. Garnish with chopped parsley. Serves 4.

Mint and Fruit Punch
1700 recipe of President James Monroe

½ cup water
⅓ cup sugar
½ cup mint leaves, divided
1 cup grape juice
1 cup orange juice
½ cup lemon juice

Boil water and remove from stove. Add sugar and ¾ of the mint leaves. Stir the mixture until the sugar is dissolved. When cool, strain out the mint; add grape, orange, and lemon juice. Chill overnight and serve over ice with a mint leaf on top. Serves 4 to 6.

Coleslaw

4 cups cabbage, shredded
½ cup mayonnaise
2 tablespoons lemon juice
1 tablespoon grated onion
½ teaspoon celery seed
1 teaspoon sugar
½ teaspoon salt
⅛ teaspoon pepper
Paprika
Green onion rings (slice green portion about ⅛-inch thick)

Shred cabbage and place in ice water. Combine mayonnaise, lemon juice, onion, celery seed, sugar, salt, and pepper. Drain cabbage and mix with dressing. Serve in lettuce cups. Garnish with a dash of paprika and green onion rings. Serves 6 to 8.

Deviled Eggs

6 hard-boiled eggs, halved
½ teaspoon salt
½ teaspoon black pepper
½ teaspoon dry mustard
2 teaspoons parsley, minced
2 tablespoons chopped sweet pickles
3 tablespoons mayonnaise
Paprika

Remove egg yolks; set egg whites aside. Mash egg yolks and mix with remaining ingredients except paprika. Fill egg halves with mixture and garnish with a sprinkling of paprika. Refrigerate. Serve cold.

How many Shrimp are in a Pound?

The commercial seafood industry doesn't know either. The terms Small, Medium, Large, X-Large, and Jumbo are grocery store terms. These terms have no standard meaning and are useless. The shrimp industry grades shrimp by separating shrimp by size and the number of shrimp per pound. Use these counts to comparative shop and save money. A good-size shrimp for all-around frying and cooking grades 26 to 30 per pound (large). Medium (36 to 40 per pound) are good for gumbo and boiling. Small (50 to 60 per pound) are usually purchased cooked, peeled, and bagged. X-Jumbo (10 to 15 per pound) are "baby lobsters." Most raw shrimp that we purchase are harvested from the Gulf of Mexico. Of the three kinds of shrimp harvested in the gulf, 57% are brown shrimp, 34% white shrimp, and 9% are pink shrimp. White shrimp are the premium shrimp because of their mild flavor. Brown shrimp are more plentiful, but they have a stronger flavor due to their higher iodine count. Pink shrimp are relatively rare and if they can be found, they are expensive. Cook raw shrimp within one to two days of purchase and they may be refrigerated for another two to three days. If you buy shrimp in quantity, frozen raw headless shrimp will maintain their quality longer than cooked shrimp. It is important not to over-cook shrimp as they will become dry and rubbery. Cook only until the flesh is white and slightly firm.

Cold Shrimp-Dill Appetizer

1 cup mayonnaise
2 tablespoons bottled chili sauce
½ onion small, minced
½ garlic clove, minced
6 fresh stalks dill, finely chopped
1 teaspoon celery seed
2 stalks celery with leaves, finely chopped
2 pounds (medium-sized, 36 to 40 per pound) shrimp, shelled and boiled

Combine all ingredients, adding shrimp last. Can be made the day before and refrigerated. Serve with crackers.

Cold Shrimp and Cucumber Potato Salad

4 medium potatoes, ¾-inch pieces
1 tablespoon rice wine vinegar
2 tablespoons Dijon mustard
⅓ cup olive oil
1 tablespoon finely chopped fresh dill
4 green onions, white and green chopped
Salt and white pepper
4 small cucumbers, halved and sliced
½ pound (small-sized, 50 to 60 per pound) shrimp, boiled and peeled

Boil potato pieces until tender and place in a large serving bowl. Whisk together vinegar and mustard; slowly whisk in olive oil. Add ½ vinegar dressing to potatoes. Add dill, onions, salt and pepper. Refrigerate 1 hour. When ready to serve, add remaining vinegar dressing, cucumbers and shrimp. Serves 4.

Quick Shrimp Newburg

1 can cream of shrimp soup
¾ cup evaporated milk
2 tablespoons dry sherry (optional)
1 (4-ounce) can mushroom slices
1½ cups (medium-sized, 36 to 40 per pound) shrimp, boiled
2 egg yolks, beaten
Cooked rice for 4

Place soup, milk, sherry, and mushrooms into boiler; mix well. Simmer until completely heated. Add shrimp and egg yolks; cook until shrimp is done. Serve hot over white rice. Serves 4.

Grecian Shrimp

3 tablespoons olive oil
2 tablespoons fresh lemon juice
Salt and pepper
1 pound (large-sized, 26 to 30 per pound) shrimp, boiled and shelled
1 medium white onion, thin-sliced rings
¼ cup sliced green olives
3 tablespoons pimento slices
1 lemon, cut into wedges

Mix olive oil, lemon juice, and salt and pepper to taste; set aside. Place boiled shrimp in the lemon/oil mixture, and mix well. Refrigerate overnight. Cover with onion rings, olives, and pimento. Serve with lemon wedges.

Summer

KEEPER BASS
MUST BE
14 INCHES
"RELEASE ALL BASS
UNDER 14"

More than one way to Skin a Catfish

Up front and for the record, I am not a catfish skinner. I had rather skin 10 deer or scale 100 bream than to try skin one old channel catfish. I don't know what it is about skinning a catfish that is so difficult for me. I have just never gotten the hang of it. I remember back in 1968, when I was given a nice seven to eight pound catfish, with the directions to nail his head up against the barn and just pull the skin off. That didn't work for me. I ended up wasting thirty minutes trying to skin the monster and then another twenty minutes "carving" it up in eating-size pieces. I can also remember back when my dad would take me fishing and he would throw back the catfish calling them trash fish. He would quickly slide a knife down the backbone, flip the fillet over and then slide the knife down between the flesh and the skin. If they were trash fish, why in heaven's name would he do this to the poor thing? I mean if you are going to eat one, that's one thing, but if you are going to throw it back as trash, throw it back, but why butcher it? What the heck did he do with it once he slaughtered it? How times have changed.

Deep-Fried Louisiana-Style Thin-Sliced Catfish

2 large whole catfish fillets
Milk
1 gallon vegetable oil
2 cups yellow cornmeal
2¼ teaspoons salt
1 teaspoon black pepper
½ teaspoon cayenne pepper (optional)

Slice fillets across the grain in ⅛- to ¼-inch thin slices. Wash the fillets under cold water and pat dry. Cover fillets with milk and set aside. Preheat oil in cooker to 375°. In a paper bag, mix together cornmeal, salt, and peppers. Dredge the fish in the cornmeal mixture, lay flat and allow to dry for a few minutes. Fry 4 to 6 pieces a time for about 5 to 7 minutes or until golden brown. Drain on paper towels and serve. Serves 4.

Skillet-Fried Whole Catfish with Wilted Spinach

3 bunches spinach
½ cup yellow cornmeal
½ cup flour
Salt
2 (1- to 1¼-pounds) whole catfish, cleaned
4 slices bacon
4 tablespoons butter
Lemon wedges

Wash spinach very thoroughly, drain, and place in the refrigerator. Mix cornmeal, flour, and salt in a paper bag and coat fish. Fry bacon and drain on paper towels. Add butter to bacon drippings, lay in fish, cover and gently fry for 15 minutes. Turn fish and fry another 15 minutes or until golden. Remove fish to a warm platter. Place spinach in the skillet, cover, and wilt. Serve spinach with lemon wedge along side of catfish. Serves 2 to 4.

Deep-fried
Louisiana catfish..

Catfish Gumbo

¼ cup vegetable oil
1½ cups chopped onion
1 cup chopped green bell pepper
1 cup chopped celery
2 cloves garlic, minced
4 cups chicken broth
1 (10-ounce) package frozen sliced okra
1 (16-ounce) can stewed tomatoes
1 teaspoon salt
¼ teaspoon cayenne pepper
½ teaspoon oregano
1 bay leaf
½ teaspoon thyme
2½ pounds catfish, 1-inch cubes
Cooked rice for 10
Filé powder

Heat oil in a pot or Dutch oven; sauté onion, bell pepper, celery, and garlic. Add broth, okra, tomatoes, salt, pepper, oregano, bay leaf, and thyme. Cover and simmer 30 minutes. Stir frequently from bottom. Add catfish chunks and simmer about 15 minutes or until flesh firms. Serve over rice with filè powder. Serves 10.

Catfish Paté

½ cup cooked catfish
1 (8-ounce) package cream cheese, softened
1 stick butter, softened
1 garlic clove, minced fine
2 tablespoons lemon juice
2 tablespoons white wine (optional)
Dash cayenne pepper

Place all ingredients in a food processor and process until smooth. Cover and chill 4 hours. Serve with crackers.

Shrimping with Shorty

Shorty Cramps was a one-man shrimping operation. He was one of the old-timers who had settled on a back bay in the early 1900's, built a house that survived hurricanes and raised his family shrimping by himself. Shorty built his boat and he built his home—with his own hands. I have not seen Shorty since the summer of 1963, but I knew him long before. Long before the area was developed and the high-rise hotels and condominiums replaced the 100-year-old pines and the scattered homes of the local fishermen. We vacationed each summer in a rustic old house on an isolated portion of a back bay. Shorty lived down the bay and at daylight of our second day, Dad would always take me over to Shorty's house and Mrs. Cramps would feed me ham and biscuits and give me milk-coffee in a heavy ceramic mug that had no handle. Dad would hire Shorty for a morning of "shrimping" and we would spend the morning dragging and sorting out a very few shrimp from a large number of catfish and stingrays. What I remember most about these vacations was Shorty kneeling down beside me and telling me the name of each new creature that I came up with. It is surprising how the little events of our youth are the ones that we remember in our maturity.

Italian Grilled Shrimp Appetizer

6 extra-large shrimp per person, peeled
1 (24-ounce) bottle Wishbone Italian salad dressing, divided
Bamboo skewers
1 cup cooked rice per person
Salt and pepper
1 tablespoon finely chopped green onions per person
1 tablespoon finely chopped black olives per person
1 tablespoon minced anchovies per person

Marinate and refrigerate shrimp in ¾ bottle dressing for 1 hour. Skewer 3 shrimp on each skewer (cut skewer to desired size); grill both sides until flesh is just barely firm basting several times with marinade. Mold each cup of rice in a ramekin, invert ramekin, and bump molded rice onto small serving plates. Season rice with salt and pepper to taste; arrange 2 shrimp skewers beside each serving of rice. Sprinkle rice and shrimp with green onions and olives. Drizzle rice with a small amount of dressing. Spoon a pinch of anchovy on the top and center of the rice.

Shrimp and Sausage Jambalaya

2 tablespoons cooking oil
1 pound venison link or other sausage, ¼-inch-thick slices
2 cups chopped onions
¾ cup chopped bell peppers
¾ cup chopped celery
Salt, black pepper and red pepper
1 cup raw white long grain rice
1 (14½-ounce) can chopped tomatoes
1 tablespoon chopped garlic
4 bay leaves
¼ teaspoon dried thyme
1 pound (medium-sized, 36 to 40) shrimp, peeled
¼ cup chopped green onions

Heat oil in a large pot or Dutch oven, add sausage and cook 2 minutes. Add onion, bell pepper and celery. Season with salt, black pepper and red pepper to taste; sauté 6 to 8 minutes or until just wilted and soft. Stir in rice. Add tomato with juice, garlic, bay leaves, thyme and 2 cups water. Cover and cook 20 minutes over medium heat. Season shrimp with salt and black pepper to taste, add to pot and cook 10 more minutes or until rice is tender, liquid is absorbed and shrimp is pink. Remove from heat and let stand covered for 5 minutes. Stir in green onion and serve. Serves 6.

Crunchy Almond Shrimp

2 eggs, lightly beaten
¼ cup cream
½ cup flour
2 garlic cloves, minced
½ teaspoon ground ginger
Tabasco sauce (optional)
1 pound (medium-sized, 36 to 40) shrimp, peeled
1 cup crushed blanched almonds

Combine eggs, cream, flour, garlic, ginger, and a few dashes of Tabasco sauce. Dip shrimp in batter; roll in crushed almonds. Fry shrimp in a deep fat fryer until golden. Serves 2 to 4.

King Fishing:
Trolling the Close-In Coastal Shores

Between high school and college, I spent several years of my misspent youth working in the offshore oil industry. My day was fairly regulated in that I had to visit each one of my oil production platforms, perform a little maintenance, and record production information. Caesar Broussard was the skipper of my boat. Some days I would finish with my work early and Caesar would break out the fishing poles. We would spend a lazy afternoon fishing for whatever was biting. One day Caesar climbed up on the platform deck to tell me he had heard on the radio that his brother-in-law Justin Bero had just caught 20 of the largest king mackerels he had ever seen and they wanted to know if we wanted any. I knew exactly what to do with

kingfish. It didn't take Caesar long to crank those big diesels, get us across those 15 miles of ocean to the drilling rig, and load six of the largest king mackerels that either Caesar or I had ever seen. Caesar claimed two and I took the other four. For the next six months, every dinner guest at 832 North Rampart Street was treated to king mackrel; every way that it could be cooked.

The rig that caught the kingfish.

Grilled Mackerel with Toasted Garlic Butter

4 ounces butter
5 garlic cloves, mashed
4 medium mackerel fillets with skin
Salt and pepper
2 limes, quartered

Preheat grill to medium and wipe grates with cooking oil. Melt butter in a saucepan, add garlic and sauté until brown. Make three diagonal cuts on the skin side of the fillet and season with salt and pepper. Place flesh-side-down on grill and cook 2 to 3 minutes. Flip fillets over and cook another 2 to 3 minutes. Remove and brush with garlic butter. Serve with lime quarters. Serves 4.

Kingfish Curry

1½ pounds king mackerel, finger-size
Red chili powder
Turmeric powder
Salt
½ cup canned mango or papaya juice
1 cup grated coconut
Turmeric powder
1 tablespoon coconut oil (can be substituted with other cooking oil)
2 medium onions, sliced
Cooking oil
Cooked rice for 2 to 4

Season fish with 1 tablespoon chili powder, a pinch of turmeric, and 1 tablespoon salt. Refrigerate 15 minutes; add juice. Process coconut with a pinch of turmeric and chili powder to taste; add water as needed to make a loose paste. Add this to the fish and mix. Boil 20 minutes or until fish is firm. Stir in coconut oil. Fry onions in a little cooking oil until brown; add to mackerel curry and serve with hot rice. Serves 2 to 4.

Mackerel Cayman

1 pound mackerel, 2- to 3-inch pieces
Salt, pepper and garlic powder
1 tablespoon cooking oil
½ green bell pepper, julienned
½ red bell pepper, julienned
½ hot pepper, chopped (optional)
1 onion, cut in strips
⅓ cup rice wine or cider vinegar

Season fish with salt, pepper and garlic powder to taste. Heat oil in a skillet and fry fish 4 to 6 minutes until lightly brown and flesh is firm. Remove to serving dish. In remaining oil, fry peppers and onion until lightly cooked. Add vinegar and bring to a boil. Pour over mackerel. Serves 6.

Grilled King Mackerel

4 (1-inch-thick) king mackerel steaks
2 cups Italian salad dressing
1 zucchini, ½-inch slices
1 yellow squash, ½-inch slices
2 carrots, 2-inch pieces halved
12 broccoli florets
4 tablespoons olive oil or butter

Cover mackerel with water and refrigerate 4 hours. Marinate steaks in Italian dressing 4 hours in refrigerator. Heat grill to medium. Divide vegetables evenly between four pieces of aluminum foil; add 1 tablespoon olive oil or butter to each. Close each foil packet. Cook vegetables until tender yet crisp. Cook mackeral until meat is firm — try to turn only once. Serves 4.

Spadefishing Southern Rigs and Reefs

I was a youngster of eleven when my dad took my mother and me in search of spadefish off the coast. That was the summer I was recovering from an automobile accident. I looked a real mess with my head wrapped in a turban bandage. But I didn't much care how I looked. We were going after the "big ones." Have you ever wondered what it would be like to tangle with a 10-pound bream? Spadefish are large silver flatfish and they are awesome fighters. They usually run in the 3- to 4-pound range and they can strip off 50 yards of line in a single run. Spadefish swim in schools around rigs and the man-made reefs that stretch across the coastal waters of the Gulf of Mexico, around Florida, and up the Georgia-Carolina coasts. Peeled shrimp and squid are both proven to catch spadefish. However, if the fish are not schooling on the surface, anchor on top of the reef or tie up to a rig and fish just off the bottom. It sometimes takes them a moment to get the bait into their small mouth, but once you feel a firm tug, set the hook, and hang on. Some anglers will slowly bring the first spadefish up to the boat and leave him in the water, as the school will sometimes follow him up. Angling for spadefish is the perfect saltwater fishing trip for youngsters. The fish are manageable, the trip out is not long or expensive, and I have seldom come back empty handed. Like king mackerel, spadefish are a little oily but exceptionally tasty.

Parmesan Baked Spadefish

2 pounds skinless spadefish fillets
2 tablespoons lime or lemon juice
3 tablespoons mayonnaise
¼ cup butter, softened
Dash Tabasco sauce
⅓ teaspoon salt
½ cup Parmesan cheese, grated
3 tablespoons chopped green onion tops

Grease a baking pan; add a single layer of fillets. Coat with lemon or lime juice, cover, and let stand 5 to 10 minutes. Combine remaining ingredients and set aside. Broil fish 8 minutes. Cover with Parmesan cheese mixture, and broil another 3 minutes until flesh is firm and flakes. Serves 6.

Tangerine Sorbet

2 tablespoons grated tangerine rind
3½ cups tangerine juice (18 to 20 tangerines)
½ cup lemon juice (3 to 4 lemons)
1¼ cups sugar
¼ cup light corn syrup
Mint sprigs for garnish

Combine all ingredients and stir until sugar dissolves. Transfer to ice cream maker and freeze according to manufacturer's instructions. Pack into a freezer container and place in the freezer until set, 2 to 4 hours. Scoop into chilled wine glasses, garnish with mint, and serve immediately.

Sautéed Spadefish and Scallops

1 tablespoon plus 1 teaspoon butter, divided
1 tablespoon flour plus more for dusting
Olive oil
Salt and pepper
2 pounds spadefish fillets
2 slices bacon, chopped
½ pound scallops
1 tablespoon lemon juice
1 teaspoon cooking oil
1 pint cream

Melt 1 tablespoon butter; mix in 1 tablespoon flour then refrigerate to firm. Heat a sauté pan and add ⅛-inch olive oil. Salt and pepper fillets; dust with flour. Sauté 3 minutes on medium heat, turn and sauté another 3 minutes. Remove to platter. Cook bacon until brown and remove pieces from pan. Add 1 teaspoon butter, salt and pepper to taste, scallops and lemon juice; sauté 2 to 3 minutes. Remove scallops; add cooking oil and scrape bottom of skillet. Add cream and refrigerated butter/flour mixture; cook and stir until sauce begins to thicken. Pour over fish and scallops. Serves 6.

Trash Fish or Southern Comfort

Trotline fishing is my favorite way to fish for a traditional staple of the southern diet—catfish. Catfish can be found anywhere from roadside ditches and creeks to ponds, large lakes, muddy rivers, and small creeks. There was a time when the catfish was called a trash fish and was either thrown on the bank or given away to the country folk. However, my granddad was one who kept, fried, and loved his catfish as much as he did his Southern Comfort. It was he who taught me how to run a trotline, how to fry cornmeal-crusted catfish, and how to make moist and soft hushpuppies. We baited a lot of trotlines in the dim light of those hot summer evenings. We tied them across small coves or strung them from tree limbs along a bank. For a little boy, it was a big thrill to lift up the line and feel the fight of a catfish deep in the muddy water. We preferred to use live bait and we would seine the shallow end of the lake and catch enough little 3-inch bream to bait up the hooks. We never skinned our catch. The small ones we tossed back and the keepers we filleted. What was once a well-kept secret of the southern country folk can now be found on the menus of some of the best restaurants in the world.

Southern Fried Catfish

Oil for frying
¾ cup yellow cornmeal
¼ cup all-purpose flour
¼ teaspoon garlic powder
2 teaspoons salt
1 teaspoon red or black pepper or to taste
1½ pounds catfish fillets, cut to portions
Tomato slices and parsley sprigs for garnish

Fill a deep pot or a large skillet ½ full of oil and heat to 350°. Mix the next 5 ingredients in a paper sack. Drop in fillets and shake to cover. Add a few pieces at a time to the hot oil and fry until golden brown. Drain on paper towels. Serves 4 to 6.

Pappy's Hushpuppies

(Adapted from a recipe by Mr. Carlton Allen.)

5 pounds white onions, chopped
6 green bell peppers, chopped
1½ cups sugar
2 teaspoons cayenne pepper
2 cups self-rising flour
10 cups self-rising cornmeal
½ cup white vinegar
4 eggs, beaten
Peanut oil

To make batter, mix chopped onions and bell peppers. Purée, in batches, in a food processor until liquefied; set aside. Sift together sugar, pepper, flour, and cornmeal. Combine onion/pepper mixture, sifted dry ingredients, vinegar and egg; cover and refrigerate overnight. Heat peanut oil in a deep-fat fryer or a large cast iron cooking pot until oil reaches 375°. Drop heaping tablespoons of dough into heated oil and cook until golden brown. Do not crowd hushpuppies as they will swell while cooking. Fry in batches and allow to drain between layers of paper towels. Serves 30 to 40 (half recipe to make hushpuppies for 10 to 20 people).

Serving up Pappy's
Hushpuppies.

Orange-Poached Catfish Fillets

1 tablespoon vegetable oil
2 tablespoons diced red onion
1 teaspoon chopped fresh rosemary
¼ cup fresh orange juice
¼ teaspoon grated orange rind
1½ pounds catfish fillets, cut to portions
½ teaspoon salt or to taste
⅛ teaspoon white or black pepper or to taste
Orange slices and rosemary sprigs for garnish

Heat skillet and then add oil. Add onion and cook until just clear; add rosemary, orange juice, and orange rind. Reduce liquid over medium heat for 1 minute. Add catfish, season to taste, cover and poach 8 to 10 minutes or until the flesh is firm. Strain sauce and spoon over fillets. Garnish with orange and rosemary. Serves 4 to 6.

Caribbean Fried Catfish

2 tablespoons minced fresh cilantro
1 tablespoon minced fresh ginger
1 garlic clove, minced
2 tablespoons vegetable oil
1½ pounds catfish fillets, cut to portions
Oil for frying
1 cup all-purpose flour
Cilantro sprigs for garnish

Mix cilantro, ginger, garlic, and vegetable oil in a bowl; add fillets, toss to coat, cover, and refrigerate overnight. Heat a large skillet and pour in frying oil. Remove fillets from marinade, pat dry, and coat with flour. Fry 3 minutes on each side or until golden and flesh is firm. Garnish with cilantro. Serves 4 to 6.

Celebrating the Fourth in Style

Americans love to cookout with family and friends. And what better way to celebrate the 4th of July than to cook on the grill? Bert Wolf wrote "Gatherings and celebrations have the ability to put us in touch with our true feeling about families, nature, and the world around us." Celebrations and eating together are the glue that binds our families and generations together. Let the children get their hands into making the Deer Spread Appetizer and Lemon/Lime Soda Pop. I can promise you they will remember making and eating these two recipes for the rest of their lives and someday they will teach their children. These recipes are simple to prepare, and except for the Grilled Redfish, can be made the day before.

Grilled Redfish with Béarnaise Sauce

2 packages instant béarnaise sauce
3 pounds redfish fillets
Olive oil
Parsley

Prepare the béarnaise sauce per directions and lay a piece of plastic wrap on the surface. Refrigerate; warm before serving. Cut fillets into serving-size pieces and coat with olive oil; place in the refrigerator. Heat grill to medium. Coat fish again with olive oil and cook on one side until just firm. Turn fish and cook until fish just flakes. Do not over-cook. Place on serving plates, cover with sauce and garnish with parsley. Serves 4 to 6.

Fresh Blackberry Sherbet

1½ cups fresh blackberries
⅓ cup powdered sugar
⅔ cup sweetened condensed milk
2 tablespoons fresh lemon juice
2 egg whites, beaten stiff

Mix blackberries with sugar and let stand 15 minutes. Press blackberries through a sieve or food mill; combine juice with condensed milk and lemon juice. Chill until mixture begins to thicken; fold in egg whites. Place in freezer until partially frozen. Remove and beat until smooth. Re-freeze until ready to serve. Serves 3 to 4.

Deer Spread Appetizer

1 pound venison, 2-inch pieces
Salt and pepper
4 stalks celery
4 green onions
8 ounces pecans or walnut pieces
1½ tablespoons mayonnaise
1 (8-ounce) package cream cheese, softened
Crackers

Place venison, salt, and pepper in a crockpot; cover with water and cook on low 8 hours. Drain and purée venison in a food processor. Remove venison; purée celery, onion, and nuts. Combine puréed venison, puréed vegetables, mayonnaise, and cream cheese; re-process until smooth. If made the day before, place plastic wrap on the surface to prevent skimming. Store in refrigerator and serve cold on crackers. Serves 20.

Lemon/Lime Soda Pop

In the 1800's, before Coca-Cola was bottled, a mixture of bicarbonate of soda and tartaric acid was added to fruit drinks to make them fizz.

4 teaspoons cream of tartar
4 cups sugar
1 quart boiling water
1 tablespoon vanilla extract
3 egg whites, beaten stiff
Lemon juice
Baking soda

Dissolve cream of tartar and sugar in boiling water. Remove from stove; add vanilla extract. When this mixture has cooled, add egg whites and stir thoroughly. Pour syrup into bottles with screw-type tops and refrigerate. To make actual soda pop, dissolve 2 tablespoons syrup plus ½ teaspoon lemon or lime juice per 8-ounce glass of ice cold water; add ½ teaspoon baking soda.

July Bass:
Fishing the Ledges and Deep Points

Successful angling for largemouth bass in July is not difficult. In the heat of the summer, bass tend to build up in schools on ledges bordering deep cooler water, on deep points, and around rock piles or structures. During the dog days of summer, the fishing location is more important than the time of day. Shad will tell you a lot about where the bass are. Shad swim in schools close to the surface and when you see a school scatter and break the water, bass have just come up to feed. Try using top water baits such as a Tiny Torpedo, Hot Shot, Pin Fish, Rattle Trap, Zara Puppy or Spook. The Carolina Rig is deadly when bass are on the bottom or near structures. A Carolina Rig is simple to build. Start with a 7- to 7 ½-foot medium-heavy pole with 17-pound test line, slip on a 1-ounce worm weight, then a red plastic bead, and tie to a #10 swivel. Tie a 3-inch length of 12-pound test line to the swivel and tie on a 1/0 offset hook with a plastic lizard, Toothpick, or French Fry plastic worms.

Lemon Pepper Bass

Vegetable oil
2 tablespoons lemon pepper
2 cups yellow cornmeal
Salt
1½ pounds bass fillets, bite-size pieces
1 egg, beaten

Heat vegetable oil in deep fryer. Mix lemon pepper, cornmeal, and salt to taste. Dip bass into egg then dredge in cornmeal mixture. Cook fish in small batches until golden brown. Serves 2 to 4.

Bass Amandine

¼ pound butter
4 tablespoons almond slivers
1 lemon, halved
2 pounds bass fillets
Salt and pepper

Melt butter. Add almonds and juice from ½ lemon; cook until almonds begin to turn. Remove almonds and juice. Lay in fillets; cover with juice of ½ lemon and salt and pepper to taste. Cook on both sides until flesh is firm. Cover with almonds and butter-juice.

Southern Fried Bass

1½ pounds bass fillets, 1-inch wide strips
1 quart buttermilk
1 quart cooking oil
Salt and pepper
1 pound yellow cornmeal

Soak bass 1 hour in buttermilk. Heat cooking oil in a deep fat fryer. Mix salt, pepper, and cornmeal. Coat bass with cornmeal mixture. Fry in small batches until golden brown. Serves 2 to 4.

Spicy Bass Jerky

1 pound bass fillets
1 cup onion rings, cut in half
½ cup orange juice
1 tablespoon jalapeño pepper, finely chopped
1 tablespoon soy sauce
1 tablespoon minced garlic
2 tablespoons dark brown sugar
1 teaspoon salt
1 teaspoon fresh grated ginger
¼ teaspoon black pepper

Cut fillets into ¼- to ½-inch wide strips. Mix remaining ingredients together, add bass, and refrigerate 4 hours. Place bass in a dehydrator until firm. Or, run a string in the hot attic and hang bass from opened paperclips. The attic heat should dehydrate fish in two days.

Oven Baked Bass

2 pounds bass fillets
6 ounces (12 tablespoons) teriyaki sauce
Lemon juice
Lemon pepper
1 medium white onion, sliced thin
1 tablespoon chopped fresh cilantro

Marinate bass 1 hour in teriyaki sauce. Line a large baking dish or pan with foil and lay in fillets. Sprinkle with lemon juice and lemon pepper; top with onion slices. Cover with foil and bake at 375° 20 minutes or until flesh is firm. Sprinkle with cilantro and serve hot.

The Last of the Winter's Venison

The freezer is beginning to look a little meat-bare as it begins filling with the fresh produce from the garden and fruit from the orchard. Here and there tucked away in deep corners of the freezer, between the fresh zucchini, this year's crappie, and behind yesterday's bass are the remains of last year's deer season: one doe loin in a stained paper wrapper. Four vacuum packages of spicy, smoked link sausage for me, one package of mild breakfast sausage for Miss Anne, 15 pounds of boneless venison stew meat destined to be made into hamburger for the Labor Day cookout at Oak Grove and two tattered packages of unknown origin and questionable contents. We plan our year around our vegetable, fruit, fish, and game harvests. The special care and extra time that we take in packaging our harvests pays us dividends in the end. It is very seldom that we have any packages lost to freezer burn. We can be thankful that the deer we harvested last season has given sustenance to our family, friends, and guests for the last year. Which reminds me, bow season is only four months away. Next month I will need to begin thinking about practicing; if I could only remember where I put my broad heads.

Broiled Venison Steak in Ketchup and Mustard Sauce

¼ cup vegetable oil
¼ cup apple cider vinegar
¼ cup ketchup
1 tablespoon Worcestershire sauce
2 cloves garlic, minced
½ teaspoon each dry mustard and salt
⅛ teaspoon black pepper
4 venison steaks, ¾-inch thick
Parsley sprigs for garnish

Combine oil, vinegar, ketchup, Worcestershire, garlic, and spices. Pour into 1-gallon resealable plastic bag; add steaks. Marinate 6 hours in refrigerator, turning every 2 hours. Remove steaks (reserving marinade) and allow to drain. Broil steaks 6 to 8 minutes per side. Cook to rare or no more than medium rare. Brush with marinade several times during cooking. While steaks are cooking, pour marinade in a saucepan and boil 10 minutes; strain and use as sauce. Place steaks on serving plates, spoon over with sauce and garnish with parsley sprigs. Serves 4.

Apple and Venison Sausage Omelet

Topping:
½ pound venison breakfast sausage
½ cup applesauce
1 tablespoon chopped pimento
½ teaspoon chopped parsley

Cook venison sausage in a skillet until browned. Drain; reserve 1 tablespoon drippings to prepare French Omelet. Crumble sausage with applesauce and set aside.

French Omelet:
4 eggs
¼ cup milk
½ teaspoon salt
Dash black pepper
1 teaspoon sausage drippings

Mix eggs, milk, salt, and pepper with a fork. Heat drippings in an omelet pan or skillet until just hot enough to sizzle a drop of water. Pour in egg mixture. Carefully draw cooked portions at the edges toward center so uncooked portions flow to bottom. Slide pan rapidly back and forth to keep eggs in motion and sliding freely. While top of omelet is still soft and creamy spread sausage mixture over half of the omelet. With pancake turner fold omelet in half turn out to a serving plate. Garnish with pimento and parsley. Serves 2.

Broiled Venison Steaks with Bacon Strips

Venison round or loin steaks, 1-inch thick
Butter, melted
Lime juice
Bacon strips

Spray broiling pan with non-stick cooking spray. Baste venison steaks with butter and lime juice. Cover with bacon strips. Place in pan and broil in the oven approximately 5 to 7 minutes per side for medium rare to medium. When you turn steaks, baste and lay on more bacon strips.

Light up the Grill and Cook the Venison Lightly

Cooking venison lightly is a must for tender and juicy grilled or broiled thick-cut (1¼-inch) steaks and whole loins. An internal temperature of 138 degrees is the goal. This temperature allows the venison to be fully cooked and still be tender and juicy. Due to a lack of fat, if venison is cooked past this temperature it will go from medium rare to shoe leather without ever passing through medium. For many, this may seem a little on the rare side, but an old chefs trick will take care of that. Insert a meat thermometer and when 138° is reached, remove the venison, wrap it in aluminum foil and set aside for 10 minutes before serving. During this resting period, the heat will continue to cook the venison to medium. The juices will remain in place when the meat is cut and it will be the tenderest venison you have ever put in your mouth. Not mushy soft, but firm and tender. There will be a pleasant and slightly pink color in the center with a gradual browning out to the edge. This technique can also be used for baked roasts.

Venison Loin with Bourbon and Green Peppercorn Sauce

1 tablespoon green peppercorns
3 ounces bourbon
2 tablespoons butter
Salt and pepper to taste
4 venison loin fillets, 1¼-inch
1 green onion, chopped
¼ cup dry red wine or grape juice
¼ cup cream
1 tablespoon chopped, mixed fresh parsley and thyme plus more for garnish

Soak peppercorns in bourbon 1 hour. Melt butter in skillet. Rub salt and pepper into venison and quickly sauté until brown on outside and rare on inside. Remove and wrap in foil. Add onions to skillet, stir in peppercorns and bourbon; boil 1 minute. Add wine and cream; reduce until it coats the back of a spoon. Add herbs and sauté for a moment. Spoon sauce on individual plates, place venison and garnish. Serves 4.

Venison T-Bone with Lemon-Mushroom Sauce

3 tablespoons lemon juice
4 venison T-bone steaks, 1-inch thick
Salt and pepper
1 teaspoon bacon drippings
2 tablespoons minced green onions
¼ pound mushrooms, sliced thin
½ garlic clove, minced
½ cup plus 1 tablespoon red wine or grape juice, divided
1 teaspoon meat extract (optional)
½ bay leaf
1 teaspoon butter, melted
1 teaspoon flour
1 tablespoon red wine or grape juice
Parsley sprigs for garnish

Pour lemon juice over steaks and set aside for 10 minutes. Drain and sprinkle with salt and pepper. Heat drippings in a skillet; sauté steaks until just brown on both sides. Remove, wrap in foil and set aside. Sauté onions until just browned. Add mushrooms and garlic; sauté until mushrooms firm. Add ½ cup wine, meat extract and bay leaf. Bring to a boil and simmer 5 minutes. Place steaks in pan and heat for 3 minutes; remove to plates. Add butter, flour and 1 tablespoon wine to skillet; mix and heat. Pour over steaks and garnish with parsley. Serves 4.

Grilled Venison Round Steak

1 cup canola oil
⅔ cup apple cider vinegar
2 tablespoons Worcestershire sauce
½ medium onion, finely chopped
½ teaspoon each salt and sugar
½ teaspoon each dried basil, dried marjoram, and dried rosemary
3 pounds boneless venison round steak, ½- to 2-inch cubes

Mix ingredients; refrigerate 24 hours. Skewer venison and grill rare. Wrap in foil; let rest 10 minutes. Slice and serve on French rolls. Serves 4 to 6.

Striped Bass Hunt Upstream

Like trout, striped bass hunt upstream. They are anadromous, meaning they live in salt water but return to fresh water to spawn. Spawning begins when the water temperature reaches 60 degrees. And depending on where you live, the annual migration to their spawning sites may be from as early as February into June or July. Striped bass have been introduced into numerous inland lakes and reservoirs and in these land-locked waters, the populations will complete their whole life cycle in fresh water. Being voracious feeders, they will consume any kind of small fish, such as shiners and minnows and a variety of invertebrates. At spawning time, running water is necessary to keep the eggs in motion until hatching, thus when fishing during the spawning season, you will improve your chance by allowing your bait to drift down stream. Regarding bait, striped bass have a very acute sense of smell and can sniff danger from bait that has been handled. I have seen old pros wearing thin rubber gloves to keep from passing their scent on to the bait.

Broiled Striped Bass with Chili and Butter Sauce

¼ cup butter, softened
½ teaspoon chili powder
¼ teaspoon cumin
⅛ teaspoon red pepper
1 garlic clove, minced
2 pounds striped bass fillets
4 large flour tortillas, warmed
Refried beans for 4
Salsa
Cilantro sprigs for garnish

Place first 5 ingredients in a bowl and mix together. Coat fillets with chili-butter and broil 5 to 7 minutes or until the flesh is firm. Place a tortilla on each serving plate and lay a fillet across the center. Place refried beans on one side and salsa on the other side. Garnish with cilantro. Serves 4.

Italian Baked Striped Bass

2 pounds striped bass fillets
1 cup sour cream
1 tablespoon fresh lemon juice
¼ cup grated Parmesan cheese
2 tablespoons chopped green onions
⅛ teaspoon Tabasco sauce
⅛ teaspoon paprika
Fresh parsley sprigs for garnish

Preheat oven to 350°. Coat a baking dish with cooking spray. Slice fillets into individual servings and lay in dish. Mix together sour cream, lemon juice, cheese, onions, and Tabasco sauce; spoon over fillets. Sprinkle on paprika. Bake in the oven for 15 minutes or until flesh is firm. Garnish with parsley and serve. Serves 4 to 6.

Spicy Striped Bass Creole

1 tablespoon fresh grated ginger
1 tablespoon ground coriander
1 tablespoon cumin
1 tablespoon curry powder
1 teaspoon dried basil leaves
¼ teaspoon cayenne pepper (optional)
4 tablespoons olive oil
2 onions, chopped
3 tablespoons minced garlic
4 tablespoons flour
2 cups chicken stock or canned broth
2 tablespoons butter
1 fresh jalapeño pepper, seeded, chopped
Salt and pepper
2 pounds striped bass fillets, ½-inch cubes
Cooked egg noodles for 4 to 6

Preheat oven to 350°. Mix herbs and spices together and set aside. Heat oil in a large, deep casserole dish and sauté onions and garlic until onions are just clear. Whisk flour into stock and add to onions along with butter, jalapeño and salt and pepper to taste. Bring to a boil and reduce until slightly thickened. Add fish cubes, remove from heat, cover and bake 10 minutes. Serve over egg noodles. Serves 4 to 6.

Fresh, Frozen, or Fresh Frozen

The "fresh" shrimp that you purchase in the average supermarket has been frozen and thawed. Almost all shrimp are frozen before being shipped. On large trawlers, shrimp are processed, packaged, and frozen at sea. Fresh shrimp that have never been frozen are usually only available in coastal areas, purchased directly off the smaller shrimp boats or from shrimp trucks which make daily trips to the coast and purchase unfrozen shrimp directly off the trawlers. Whether fresh, frozen, or fresh frozen, look for shrimp that are firm, and have a fresh smell. Purchase ½ pound of headless shrimp per serving. Avoid shrimp with dark spots, soft or loose shells, or strong odor. Rinse shrimp with cool water before placing them in your refrigerator and cook within two days. Always thaw frozen shrimp in the refrigerator or in cold water — never on the counter or under warm water.

Shrimp Scampi

1 teaspoon butter
2 teaspoons olive oil
3 cloves garlic, minced
1 pound (36 to 40) medium headless shrimp
¼ cup white wine
Juice of 1 lemon
¼ teaspoon salt
¼ teaspoon pepper
Cooked noodles or rice for 6
¼ cup finely chopped parsley
Lemon wedges

Melt butter and oil together in a sauté pan. Add garlic and sauté 1 minute. Add shrimp; sauté another minute. Add wine, lemon juice, salt, and pepper. Sauté quickly while sauce reduces and shrimp turn pink. Do not overcook, as shrimp will become tough. Serve over noodles or rice, sprinkle with parsley and garnish with lemon wedges. Serves 6.

Curried Shrimp Puffs

¾ pound (small-sized, 50 to 60 per pound) small shrimp, peeled
1 tablespoon butter
3 tablespoons minced onion
1 tablespoon curry powder
1 cup cream
3 tablespoons fine cut chutney
Salt and pepper
24 cream puffs

Chop shrimp into ¼- to ½-inch pieces and set aside. Melt butter and sauté onion until clear; stir in curry powder. Add cream and chutney and reduce to ½ cup. Add salt and pepper to taste and shrimp; cook 1 to 2 minutes and no more. Slice off tops from cream puffs and fill with shrimp mixture. Replace tops and serve.

Coconut Battered Shrimp

2 cups cooking oil
6 x-large shrimp (or 10 to 15 large)
1 teaspoon Creole powder
¼ cup flour
1 egg beaten with 2 tablespoons water
1 cup shredded coconut
1 tablespoon honey
2 tablespoons Creole mustard

Heat oil to 360°. Sprinkle shrimp with Creole powder. Dredge shrimp in flour and then dip completely in beaten egg. Dredge in coconut and press on shreds. Sauté shrimp until brown on all sides; drain. Combine honey and mustard; spoon over shrimp. Serves 2.

Shrimp and Broccoli Casserole

½ cup butter
⅓ cup chopped onion
1 pound (medium-sized, 36 to 40) shrimp peeled
¾ teaspoon chopped fresh tarragon leaves
2 tablespoons chopped parsley
2 tablespoons lemon juice
½ teaspoon salt
Cooking oil
2 (10-ounce) packages frozen broccoli, cooked
¼ cup grated Parmesan cheese
¼ cup fine cornflake crumbs
Lemon and tomato wedges for garnish

Preheat oven to 350°. Melt butter and sauté onions until clear. Add shrimp, heat until warm, and set aside. Add tarragon, parsley, lemon juice, and salt. Grease 6 (10-ounce) ramekins and divide broccoli between. Divide shrimp between ramekins. Mix together cheese and cornflakes and divide between. Bake 12 to 15 minutes. Serve with lemon and tomato. Serves 6.

Ambushed by a Flounder

Adult flounder enter shallow water, under the cover of darkness, where they lie partially buried in sand or mud waiting to ambush small fish as they swim by. There are over 200 known species of flounder worldwide. It is the southern flounder that is so sought after by anglers and so delicious in restaurants. Most of the flounder we eat are coincidental catches made by shrimpers while dragging the bottom for shrimp. Because shrimpers must ice down their shrimp as soon as they are caught, the flounder are also iced and arrive at the fish dock as fresh as the shrimp. When selecting flounder for stuffing, look for fish in the 1½- to 2-pound range. The eyes should be clear, the flesh firm and they should have very little "fishy" smell. Flounder for filleting should be in the 3- to 4-pound range.

Flounder Amandine

5 tablespoons butter, divided
1 tablespoon olive oil
1½ pounds flounder fillets
2 eggs, lightly beaten
Flour
¼ cup slivered almonds
¼ cup dry white wine or sparkling grape juice
1 tablespoon plus 2 teaspoons fresh lemon juice
2 teaspoons fresh lime juice
Cilantro sprigs

Melt 4 tablespoons butter and 1 tablespoon olive oil in a skillet. Dip fillets in egg and then in flour. Sauté on both sides until golden. Remove, cover and set aside. Melt remaining 1 tablespoon butter in skillet, add almonds and sauté for 1 minute. Scrape up bits from pan. Add wine and juices and reduce until thickened. Place fillets on serving plates, cover with sauce and garnish with cilantro. Serves 4.

Spinach-Stuffed Flounder Fillets

12 flounder fillets, halved long-ways
1 tablespoon lemon juice
Salt and pepper
½ cup frozen spinach, cooked and squeezed
⅛ teaspoon fresh ground nutmeg
2 eggs, separated
½ cup cream, divided
12 large raw shrimp, shelled
12 natural wooden toothpicks
¼ cup dry white wine or sparkling grape juice
2 green onions, chopped
¼ pound mushrooms, sliced thin
2 tablespoons butter
2 tablespoons flour
1 cup fish stock or canned chicken broth

Place ½ the fillets and 1 tablespoon lemon juice in a re-sealable bag, season with salt and pepper, and refrigerate. Process remaining fillets until smooth. Add spinach, salt and pepper to taste and nutmeg; process 30 seconds. While processing, pour in egg whites. Cover and chill 2 hours. Preheat oven to 350°. Mix 2 tablespoons cream into spinach and spoon 1 tablespoon of the mixture on each of the 12 chilled fillets. Lay a shrimp on top and roll. Secure with a toothpick. Grease a baking dish and stand up rolled flounders. Pour in wine, cover and bake 25 minutes. Sauté green onions and mushrooms in butter until onions are just clear. Whisk flour into stock and stir into onions until thickened. Stir egg yolks into remaining cream and mix into sauce. Bring sauce to a boil and spoon over fillets. Serves 6.

Barbecued Whole Flounder

4 (1½- to 2-pound) flounder
½ cup flour
¼ cup cooking oil
Lemon pepper
Tabasco sauce
¼ cup minced fresh parsley
4 lemon wedges

Clean, scale and wash flounder under cold water. Make a paste from flour, oil, and lemon pepper and Tabasco sauce to taste. Coat flounder inside and out with paste. Place on a preheated charcoal grill and cook 6 to 8 minutes on each side. Remove to serving plates, sprinkle with parsley and garnish with lemon wedges. Serves 4.

Baking the Big Red Fish

Anne and I love redfish. But scaling a large redfish is no easy task. With scales the size of a 25-cent piece, it is almost impossible to scale the beast in the traditional manner. When I must have a whole fish or fillets with skin, I purchase it at my supermarket. Or, you can arm yourself with a pair of pliers, sit down at a strong comfortable table, open your favorite adult beverage, and pull the scales out one-by-one. My good friend Jim slices off the fillets and leaves the scales on. He calls the fillets "Redfish on the Half-Shell" and he grills them scale side down until the top flesh is firm. My usual method of preparing redfish is to fillet down almost to the tail, flip the fillet over the tail and slice under and between the skin and the flesh. Redfish frequently weigh over 10 pounds and it is not uncommon to land one weighing 20 pounds or more. Fillets from this size fish are prime candidates for baking.

Crab-Stuffed Redfish Fillets

4 (2x3-inch) redfish fillets, 1 to 1½ inches thick
2 cups white wine
Olive oil
4 tablespoons crabmeat
1 lemon, juiced
2 teaspoons chopped fresh oregano
1 garlic clove, minced
4 thick-sliced bacon strips, halved

Preheat oven to 350°. Butterfly fillets and refrigerate in wine 3 hours. Pat dry and cover with olive oil. Place 1 tablespoon crabmeat on each fillet, fold over and seal with a wooden toothpick. Place fillets in a baking dish; sprinkle with lemon juice, oregano, and garlic. Lay bacon on top, cover with foil, and bake 30 minutes or until flesh is firm. Remove foil and place under broiler until bacon crisps. Serves 4.

Baked Creole Redfish

7 tablespoons butter, divided
1 cup thin-sliced onion
1 teaspoon minced garlic
3 cups chopped celery
3 cups chopped bell pepper
Salt and pepper
¼ cup chopped parsley
2 cups peeled, seeded, chopped tomato
2 tablespoon drained capers
Tabasco sauce
1¾ pounds redfish fillets, serving-size pieces

Preheat oven to 450°. Melt 6 tablespoons butter in a hot skillet; add onion, and sauté until just clear. Add garlic, celery, bell pepper, and salt and pepper to taste; sauté 2 minutes. Stir in parsley, tomatoes, capers and Tabasco to taste. Cover and cook 5 minutes over medium heat. Place fillets in a buttered baking dish, cover with vegetables, and bake 15 minutes. Serves 4.

Redfish with Crawfish Sauce

1 (2-pound) redfish fillet
Olive oil
Salt and red pepper
½ cup chopped onion
1 garlic clove, minced
3 tablespoons butter
½ pound crawfish tails, cooked
¼ cup milk
1 tablespoon sour cream
1 teaspoon minced fresh oregano
1 teaspoon minced fresh basil
1 teaspoon lemon juice
¼ cup white wine (optional)

Preheat oven to 400°. Cover fillets with olive oil and season with salt and red pepper to taste. Bake 10 to 15 minutes or until flesh is firm. Sauté onion and garlic in butter; add crawfish tails and warm. Stir in milk and sour cream. Add remaining ingredients and reduce sauce to ½. Pour sauce over fillet. Serves 4.

Sautéed Lime-Crusted Redfish

2 limes, divided
2 tablespoons minced parsley
1½ cups unseasoned breadcrumbs
Salt, red and black pepper
1¾ pounds redfish fillets, serving-size pieces
2 eggs, beaten
2 tablespoons olive oil
2 tablespoons butter

Grate the rind of one lime and mix with parsley, breadcrumbs; add salt, red pepper, and black pepper to taste. Dip fillets into egg and then dredge in breadcrumb mixture. Add oil and butter to a hot skillet and sauté until browned on both sides. Quarter both limes and use for garnish. Serves 4.

Miss Anne and the "Happy Snapper"

The picture is pinned to the kitchen wall. The picture is of Anne and the biggest fish she ever caught; a 4 ½ pound red snapper that she hooked on the party boat the "Happy Snapper." Party or "head" boats are coastal fishing boats that cater specifically to individuals, families with children, and walk-ons. The trips are inexpensive, casual, and are geared towards catching the species of fish that are biting that day. All fishing supplies are furnished which includes a deck hand to help with baiting your hooks, removing fish, and cleaning your catch at the dock. July is a premier month for red snapper and their range extends from Texas, around Florida and up through the Carolinas. The average size snapper weighs 3 to 5 pounds but 20 pounders are not uncommon. The fishing day will be spent anchored and bottom fishing at 60 to 100 feet for red snapper and whatever else is biting. When you feel a nibble, don't pull up on the rod as your line will have a bow in it and the fish will feel the tug and spit out the bait. Reel in hard; the fish will set the hook. If fishing for red snapper is not in your immediate plans, some of the more than eight million pounds of snapper harvested by commercial fishermen will end up in your supermarket as whole fish or fillets.

Miss Anne and her
"happy" snapper.

Baked Pineapple Snapper

4 (6-ounce) red snapper fillets
1 can pineapple pieces, drained
2 limes, juiced
4 tablespoons butter, softened
Salt and pepper

Lay fillets on foil. Combine pineapple, lime, and butter; place on fish. Salt and pepper to taste. Seal in foil and bake 20 to 30 minutes or until the flesh flakes. Serves 4.

Stuffed Red Snapper

¾ cup finely chopped celery
¾ cup finely chopped onion
1 tablespoon butter
1½ cups cooked brown or white rice
1 cup chopped tomato (skin removed)
⅓ cup chopped fresh parsley
½ teaspoon dried thyme leaves
1 (3-pound) dressed red snapper, with head
Cotton twine or skewers

Preheat oven to 350°. Cook celery and onion in butter until tender. Add cooked rice, tomato, parsley, and thyme. Lightly stuff fish; seal with cotton twine or skewers. Spray a baking dish with non-stick spray, place fish, and cover with foil. Bake 50 to 60 minutes or until flesh is firm. Serves 8.

Red Snapper Caribbean

2 pounds red snapper fillets
2 tablespoons lemon juice
2 tablespoons orange juice
2 teaspoons grated orange rind
¼ cup grated onion
½ teaspoon salt
⅛ teaspoon ground nutmeg
White pepper

Preheat oven to 350°. Cut fillets into 6 portions and place skin down in a greased 12x8-inch baking dish. Combine lemon and orange juice, orange rind, onion, and salt; pour over fillets. Refrigerate 30 to 45 minutes. Sprinkle on ⅛ teaspoon nutmeg and pepper to taste. Bake 20 to 30 minutes or until flesh is firm. Serves 6.

Steamed Red Snapper

Salt and pepper
2 (6-ounce) red snapper fillets
¼ teaspoon grated ginger
½ teaspoon chopped fresh cilantro
3 shiitake mushroom caps, thin strips or ¾ cup button mushrooms
1 green onion top, thin strips
2 tablespoons peanut oil, heated very hot
2 tablespoons soy sauce or to taste

Place a bamboo steamer or colander with a tight-fitting top over a large pot of boiling water. Salt and pepper fillets to taste. Steam snapper until flesh is firm and flaky. Place fillets on a serving plate and cover with remaining ingredients. Serves 2.

Dodging Mosquitoes & Wet Popping Bugs

At the time it was not memorable, but with the passing of many years, I now look back on these moments as some of my most treasured memories. I didn't know then, but I was learning how to fly fish, from a self-taught professional. After closing down the work-site for the day, Dad would gather me up, "recruit" Sam his truck driver and they would load up the wooden boat into the back of Dad's station wagon. Off we would go like a herd of gypsies to some remote delta ox bow lake and spend the late evening with Sam paddling while Dad fly fished for bream and I would sit on the wet bottom of the boat smelling of citronella, eating a banana that Dad gave me and dodging mosquitoes and wet popping bugs. Little did Dad know that bananas attract mosquitoes. After fishing and loading the boat, Dad would take us into the rickety bait store (sitting half on land and half over the water) sit me on the counter and feed me pickled eggs from a gallon jar and saltine crackers washed down with a Grapette soda. Dad and Sam would drink a beer, talk about the next day's work and sample the pickled pigs feet from another gallon jar. How Dad found these old, hidden lakes I never knew. I should have asked, but a seven-year-old doesn't think to ask these things.

Fried Bluegill in Lemon Batter

1 cup flour plus more for coating
2 teaspoons grated lemon zest
½ teaspoon salt
¼ teaspoon black pepper
1 cup water
1½ pounds cleaned bluegills
Cooking oil

Combine 1 cup flour, lemon zest, salt, and pepper. Slowly whisk in water. Refrigerate 30 minutes to chill. Heat cooking oil in a deep fat fryer. Dip fish in batter and fry until golden. Serves 4.

Bluegill and Macaroni Casserole

1 cup raw macaroni
1 (3-ounce) package cream cheese, softened
1 (10-ounce) can cream of mushroom soup
1½ cups cooked bluegill meat
¼ teaspoon salt
2 tablespoons prepared yellow mustard
¼ cup chopped green bell pepper
¼ cup chopped onion
¼ cup whole milk
½ cup crumbled cornflakes
¼ cup minced fresh parsley

Preheat oven to 375°. Cook macaroni per package directions and set aside to drain. Process together cream cheese and mushroom soup. Mix in the cooked macaroni and all the remaining ingredients except cornflakes and parsley. Turn out mixture into a large casserole dish and bake 20 to 25 minutes. Remove and sprinkle with cornflakes and parsley. Serves 4.

Bluegill Cocktail Salad

8 cleaned bluegill
Lettuce leaves
Cocktail sauce
1 tablespoon crabmeat
1 tablespoon prepared horseradish
2 tablespoons minced fresh cilantro

Boil bluegill until meat is firm, about 5 to 7 minutes. Remove and set aside to cool. Separate meat chunks from bone, cover and chill 1 hour. Line 4 chilled cocktail glasses with lettuce. Cover bluegill chunks with cocktail sauce and spoon onto lettuce. Top each with crabmeat and horseradish. Garnish with cilantro. Serves 4.

Italian Grilled Bluegill

8 cleaned bluegill
4 tablespoons olive oil, divided
2 tablespoons chopped fresh sage
2 zucchini, quartered long-ways
3 Italian tomatoes
Capers
Parsley sprigs

Preheat grill. Make 4 deep slices on each side of bluegill and coat with 3 tablespoons olive oil. Divide sage into 8 equal portions and stuff into cavities. Grill bluegill, zucchini and tomato. Remove to serving plates and spoon on remaining olive oil. Sprinkle each with a few capers and garnish with parsley sprigs. Serves 4.

Blue Crabs in the Moonlight

Perdido Beach was once a quiet, secluded and safe place for a young boy to spend his summer vacation. The days were warm, the nights were cool and the salt water was clear and shallow in front of the old house. A short walk behind the house was a small bay with deeper and darker water. This is where we had the boathouse, the pier, and where I would place my crab nets before supper. After supper we would sit on the front porch and I would swing in the hammocks until the sun went down and the sea breeze began to blow through the pines. When it became dark, I would walk out onto the pier and begin lifting my crab nets. I never caught many crabs, but while I waited to make another round I would lay on the weathered boards, watch the stars and think about all things being possible.

Crab-Stuffed Deviled Eggs

12 eggs, hard-boiled and halved longwise
1 teaspoon Dijon mustard
2 tablespoons lemon juice
¼ cup mayonnaise
¼ teaspoon salt
¼ teaspoon Tabasco sauce or to taste
1 tablespoon minced fresh parsley
½ pound lump crabmeat
1 ounce caviar or salmon roe (optional)

Remove yolks from eggs and mash with a fork. Mix in mustard, lemon juice, mayonnaise, salt, Tabasco sauce and parsley. Stir in crabmeat. Spoon into egg whites and refrigerate 3 hours. Spoon ⅛ teaspoon caviar on top of each egg before serving. Makes 24.

Crab Quesadillas

2 tablespoons corn oil or other oil
4 large flour tortillas
6 ounces Monterey Jack cheese, shredded
1 (4-ounce) can green chilies
2 green onions, chopped
6-ounces lump crabmeat
2 tablespoons minced fresh cilantro
4 tablespoons sour cream

Heat a large skillet over medium heat and wipe with corn oil. Place 1 tortilla in skillet and sprinkle with half the cheese, chilies, onions, crabmeat and cilantro. Top with a second tortilla and cook 2 to 3 minutes or until cheese just begins to melt and bottom begins to brown. Turn and cook until brown and cheese is completely melted. Repeat for second quesadilla. Slice in half. Spoon 1 tablespoon sour cream on each half. Serves 2 to 4.

Blackened Crab Cakes

2 pounds firm-fleshed saltwater fish
1 tablespoon minced garlic
¼ pound butter, softened
Juice of 1 lemon
1 pound crabmeat
½ green onion, chopped
Blackened fish seasoning
¼ cup melted butter
Lemon wedges
Cilantro or parsley sprigs

Process fish, garlic, butter and lemon juice to make a smooth paste. Remove to a bowl. Add crabmeat and onion; mix well. Shape into 12 patties and sprinkle with blackened fish seasoning. Heat a cast iron skillet until smoking hot; char patties on both sides. Spoon melted butter over each patty and serve with lemon wedges and a cilantro sprig. Serves 6.

West Indies Crab Salad

2 cups crabmeat
4 tablespoons minced white onion
¼ teaspoon salt
¼ teaspoon white pepper
⅛ teaspoon garlic powder
4 ounces olive oil or other oil
4 ounces rice wine or white vinegar
4 ounces iced water
Shredded lettuce leaves
Cherry tomatoes, thin sliced

Place crab on the bottom of a stainless or plastic bowl and cover with onions. Add salt, pepper and garlic. Cover with oil, vinegar, and water; do not stir. Cover and refrigerate 24 hours. Mix with a fork and serve over shredded lettuce. Top with 3 tomato slices. Serves 4.

Do Frog Legs Really Taste Like Chicken?

It all depends on who you talk to. I do know several things about frog legs that are true: the meat is white, it is tender, it is clean-tasting, and it is very delicious — sort of like chicken. My first experience in catching and skinning bullfrogs was in a very un-frog-like place — the desert around Las Vegas, Nevada. About forty miles out in the desert there are tracts of grain fields which are watered by small concrete irrigation ditches. My neighbor Roger, who was also a southern boy from "South" Manitoba, Canada, and I would trek out late in the evening to gig frogs in the hot night desert air. Who else but two Southern boys, reared in the country, could come up with a scheme to gig bullfrogs in the desert. We would walk the ditches until well past midnight and it was not uncommon for us to bring home a mess of twenty to thirty frogs. To skin a bullfrog, gently cut the skin around the mid-section, use a pair of pliers to pull the skin down and off the legs. Cut the legs off where the upper joint attaches to the body and remove the feet. They do look a little like skinny chicken legs.

Pan-Fried Frog Legs with Lemon-Butter Sauce

1 cup fine cracker crumbs
½ teaspoon garlic powder
Salt and pepper
2 tablespoons milk
2 eggs
8 skinned frog legs
Cooking oil

Lemon-Butter Sauce:

½ cup butter, melted
5 teaspoons fresh lemon juice
1 teaspoon cognac (optional)

Combine cracker crumbs, garlic powder, and salt and pepper to taste. Gently beat together milk and eggs. Dip each leg in egg wash and dredge in cracker crumbs. Pan fry in ½-inch of hot oil until golden brown. In a separate bowl, combine Lemon-Butter Sauce ingredients; pour over legs before serving. Serves 4.

Frog Legs in Mushroom Sauce

6 tablespoons butter, divided
1 cup sliced button mushrooms
1 cup plus 2 tablespoons flour, divided
Salt and pepper
12 frog legs
1½ cups chicken broth
1 tablespoon sherry (optional)

Melt and bring to sizzle 4 tablespoons butter; add mushrooms, sauté both sides until just wilted, remove, and place on a platter. Place 1 cup flour and salt and pepper to taste in a paper bag and mix. Add remaining butter to pan. Add frog legs two at a time and shake to coat. Sauté until brown on all sides; remove to platter. Add remaining flour and chicken broth to pan; stir and simmer until smooth. Add sherry if desired. Serves 6.

Stewed Frog Legs

8 frog legs
4 tablespoons butter
1 tablespoon flour
2 sprigs fresh parsley, chopped
Pinch ground savory
Bay leaf
Three slices onion, halved
Salt and pepper
1 cup hot water
1 cup cream, divided
2 egg yolks

Parboil frog legs for three minutes and drain. Melt butter in a stew pot, sauté legs on both sides until just brown, sprinkle with flour and stir. Add parsley, savory, bay leaf, onions, and salt and pepper to taste. Add 1 cup hot water, and ⅔ cup cream. Boil gently until legs are tender. Remove legs and strain gravy. Beat egg yolks into remaining ⅓ cup cream and stir into gravy. Pour gravy over legs. Serves 4.

Faster than a Speeding Dove, I am not

On the first Saturday in September, morning comes early at Oak Grove. It is the sounds of Fort Sumter, Missionary Ridge, and Vicksburg all rolled into one. The early morning air is cool and the surrounding fields echo with the booms of 10 gauges and the pops of 20 gauges. If you want to sleep late, this will not be the morning. This morning is the first day of dove season and more than 90% of all the dove hunting that will be done this year will be done on this day. In many parts of the South, the first day of dove season is the traditional beginning of hunting season. Hunters, families, and friends have been gathering and hunting dove on the same fields for 75 to 100 years or more. It is a day of ritual and traditions, as traditions are still strong in the south. Today is a day for reconfirming old friendships and making new ones. The weather is pleasant and all ages and genders are represented. This year the young girls will out-number the young boys. After the hunt and after all the doves have been cleaned and iced down, there may be time for a short snooze on the porch before the barbecue lunch which is usually followed by a banquet of dove breasts in the evening. I have been watching this year's crop of doves sailing over my fields at Oak Grove for several weeks now and this year's crop seems to be above average. Sitting on my nieces shooting stool under the persimmon tree, I am reminded that it was on the dove fields of Lauderdale County that Uncle Everett tried to teach me to wing shoot — now 55 years later, I am still trying to learn.

Sautéed Dove Breast Tetrazzini

3 tablespoons butter
3 tablespoons chopped onion
⅓ cup sliced mushrooms
2 tablespoons cornstarch
½ cup chicken broth
1½ cups dove breast meat
2 ½ cups cooked angle hair spaghetti
1 cup shredded mozzarella cheese

Melt butter in a saucepan. Add onions and mushrooms; sauté over low heat until onions are just clear. Mix cornstarch into broth and whisk into onions until sauce begins to thicken. Add dove and spaghetti; heat. Transfer to a baking dish and cover with cheese. Place dish under broiler until cheese melts. Serves 4.

Dove Breasts in Cream Sauce

16 slices bacon
8 dove breasts
Salt and pepper
1½ cups cream
3 egg yolks
1 teaspoon paprika
Bacon bits for garnish

Sauté bacon until crisp, remove, and set aside to drain. In the bacon fat, sauté breasts on all sides until meat is just firm; salt and pepper to taste and remove breasts. Save 3 tablespoons of fat. Whisk together cream and egg yolks; add reserved fat. Cook, stirring frequently, over very low heat until sauce begins to thicken. Pour sauce over breasts, sprinkle with paprika, and garnish with bacon bits. Serves 4.

Dove Enchiladas

8 large flour tortillas
2 (10-ounce) cans enchilada sauce, warmed
2 tablespoons cooking oil
8 dove breasts, boned and chopped
1 small onion, chopped
2 cloves garlic, minced
3 tablespoons chopped ripe olives
1 cup shredded Cheddar cheese, divided
Whole ripe olives for garnish

Place tortillas, one at a time in warm enchilada sauce and let stand until softened; save remaining sauce. Heat oil in a skillet; sauté dove, onion, and garlic until breasts are just browned. Spoon the dove mixture on tortillas; sprinkle with chopped olives and 1 tablespoon cheese. Roll tortillas, place in a greased baking dish, cover with remaining sauce and bake at 350° for 15 minutes. Spread on remaining cheese and bake 5 more minutes. Garnish with whole olives. Serves 4.

The Stripers are Running

Striped bass are one of our most sought-after saltwater species and they are one of the largest game fish available to the near-shore angler. They range from Texas, across the Gulf States, around Florida, and up the eastern coast and weigh-in from 1 pound to over 60 pounds. The world record striped bass weights 76 pounds and was caught from a jetty. Before Europeans arrived in America, the striped bass was one of the most prolific fish on the Atlantic and Gulf Coasts. Pilgrims discovered the American version while surf-casting from the beach and used the funds generated from the sale of their catch to build the first school in New England. Over-fishing in the 1970's reduced the population to a critical level. Strict size regulations, creel limits, and a catch-and-release program have enabled them to rebound. Stripers move with the tide and the best time to fish is at night. During the blistering summer's heat, night fishing can be a pleasant change of pace. Regarding bait, check with a local bait shop because the choice of baits are long and depend on local conditions. Cut bait works, but live bait such as "pogies" or menhaden work best. Hook your bait in the head as this   is where stripers hit their prey. Handle bait carefully; stripers have a highly   developed since of smell.

Miss Anne fishes for striped bass in Florida.

Striped Bass Italiano

2 pounds striped bass fillets, skinned
¼ cup flour
½ cup olive oil, divided
¼ cup sliced green and black olives
2 tablespoons capers
1 small onion, sliced
¼ cup chopped anchovy
1 cup tomato sauce
Minced fresh parsley for garnish

Roll fillets in flour. Heat ¾ of the olive oil in a sauté pan and sauté fish gently on both sides. Remove fish, discard oil, and wipe pan. Return fish to pan; add remaining oil, olives, capers, onion, and anchovy. Cover and simmer 20 minutes. Pour on tomato sauce, cook until fish is heated through and flesh is just firm. Garnish with parsley. Serves 4 to 6.

Baked Striped Bass in Minted Vegetable Sauce

¼ cup olive oil
1 (2-pound) can whole tomatoes
4 stalks celery, sliced
1 onion, finely chopped
3 carrots, peeled and sliced
1 bunch green onions, chopped
1 garlic clove, minced
½ teaspoon dried mint leaves
Salt and pepper
Butter
2 pounds striped bass fillets, skinned
1 lemon, cut into 6 wedges

Preheat oven to 325°. Heat oil and sauté remaining ingredients, except butter, fish and lemon until just tender. Butter a baking dish or pan, add ½ vegetable mixture, place bass on top, spoon over with remaining vegetables, cover, and bake 30 minutes or until flesh is firm. Serve with lemon. Serves 4 to 6.

Striped Bass with Lemon-Asparagus Sauce

1 pound fresh asparagus
1 (1-pound) potato, peeled
4 (1-pound) striped bass fillets
Salt and pepper
2 teaspoons olive oil
2 teaspoons fresh lemon juice

Cut 1 inch off the tips of the asparagus and set aside. Slice remaining spears (across the grain) into ½-inch long pieces; boil in lightly salted water until tender. Pureé cooked asparagus pieces and 1 cup cooking water (reserve remaining cooking liquid) until smooth; set aside. Blanch asparagus tips 2 to 3 minutes in saved cooking liquid, remove and place in iced water. Slice potato lengthwise into 4 (½-inch-wide) slices; boil in salted water until just tender, remove, and set aside. Season bass with salt and pepper to taste. Heat oil in a sauté pan until very hot and sauté fillets 3 minutes on each side or until flesh is firm. Place fillets on serving plates, whisk together lemon juice and asparagus pureé, spoon over fillets, and garnish with asparagus tips. Serves 4.

One Box of Shells—One Bird in Hand

Bird hunters everywhere look forward to dove season. For some, the day will be a hunting success. For others it will be an evening with a sore shoulder and a less-than-full game bag. Sadly, I fall in with the latter group. I gauge my success on the dove field as to how many dove I bring home in relationship to how many "boxes" of shells my old Model 12 has consumed. Dove season is the first time many of my hunting buddies, J. and Mr. Will included, have been together since the closing of deer season last year. It is a time for the re-telling of old stories and a time to enjoy the fellowship of family and friends. At the old home-place where we hunt, lunch is a banquet centering around the summer's harvests and the doves of the morning. This has been the tradition all of my life, my fathers' before me and his fathers' also.

Spicy Cajun Dove Fingers Appetizers

1 cup apricot preserves
¼ cup Dijon mustard
2½ teaspoons garlic powder
2 teaspoons dried thyme
1½ teaspoons black pepper
½ teaspoon cayenne pepper or to taste
½ teaspoon white pepper
½ teaspoon salt
12 to 18 dove breasts, 1-inch strips
1 tablespoon real butter or margarine
2 tablespoons olive or other cooking oil

In a saucepan, whisk preserves and mustard; simmer 5 minutes continuing to whisk until smooth. Combine spices and dredge dove strips; sauté in melted butter and oil on all sides until just brown. Drain on paper towels. Serves 6 to 8.

Grilled Dove Breast and Orange Appetizers

12 dove breasts
2 cups fresh orange juice
12 slices bacon, halved
24 white wooden toothpicks
Ground nutmeg

Remove meat from each side of breast. Place breast pieces in orange juice; cover and marinate in refrigerator overnight. Wrap each breast half in a piece of bacon and secure with a toothpick. Grill or roast about 10 minutes or until bacon is cooked. Sprinkle with nutmeg and serve. Makes 24

Dove Breasts with Sweet and Sour Sauce

1 cup sugar
½ cup plus 1 tablespoon water, divided
½ cup white vinegar
2 tablespoons cornstarch
2 tablespoons ketchup
2 teaspoons prepared mustard
Meat from 12 dove breasts
Cooking Oil
Cooked white rice for 4 to 6

Combine sugar, ½ cup water and vinegar in a saucepan; cook until sugar dissolves. Mix cornstarch with 1 tablespoon water; stir into sugar mixture. Continue to stir until sauce thickens. Remove from stove and allow to cool for several minutes. Stir in ketchup and mustard. Sauté dove breasts in cooking oil until they just begin to firm. Add breasts to sweet and sour sauce, warm and serve over cooked rice. Serves 4 to 6.

Baked Dove Marsala

4 cups uncooked white rice
4 tablespoons butter
16 dove breasts
Juice of 1 lemon
½ teaspoon chopped rosemary
Salt and pepper
1 pound whole medium mushrooms
1 medium onion, chopped
1¼ cups Marsala wine

Sauté rice in butter until just brown. Layer a casserole dish with rice; place dove (breasts up) and sprinkle with lemon juice, rosemary, and salt and pepper to taste. Add mushrooms and onions around breasts, cover with wine. Bake 30 minutes at 350° until breasts are tender. Serves 6 to 8.

Two Eyes on the Side of Your Head

In our southern tier of states, we have two major species of flounder: the Yellow-tail Flounder (which is caught along the Atlantic coast) and the Southern Flounder (which is caught in the Gulf of Mexico). Flounders are hatched with eyes located on both sides of their heads and begin life swimming in an upright position. By the time they reach ½-inch long, the right eye has already migrated around to the left side of the head and the fish has assumed its left-side-up swimming position. The vast quantity of flounder required by restaurants and grocery stores are the incidental catches of gulf shrimpers. Besides being a premier item on the menu of all good seafood restaurants, a walking, flounder-gigging trip along the beach at night will give your children a lasting vacation memory. Whether you find a flounder or not, they will always remember walking through the cool shallow water on a moonlit night. All the equipment you need is a homemade gig pole, a battery-operated lantern, a fish stringer, and several children.

Fillet of Flounder Au Gratin

1 tablespoon butter
¼ cup unseasoned breadcrumbs
2 tablespoons dried parsley
½ teaspoon white pepper
1 pound flounder fillets
¼ cup half-and-half
4 ounces shredded Cheddar cheese

Preheat oven to 300°. Melt butter and stir in breadcrumbs, parsley, and pepper. Spray a glass baking dish with non-stick spray. Place flounder in dish; pour on half-and-half, top with cheese then crumb mixture. Cover and bake 10 minutes; uncover and bake another 10 to 15 minutes or until flesh is firm. Serves 4.

Crab-Stuffed Flounder

4 (1-pound) flounder fillets
1 cup butter
1 bell pepper, chopped
1 cup chopped celery
½ cup chopped onion
2 cloves garlic, minced
1 pound crabmeat
3 eggs, beaten
1 tablespoon chopped parsley
½ teaspoon pepper
1 cup soft breadcrumbs

Preheat oven to 350°. Cut fillets lengthwise down the center of the dark side. Cut a pocket on each side. Melt butter and sauté pepper, celery, onion, and garlic until softened. Mix in remaining ingredients, stuff flounder, place on oiled pans and bake 30 to 40 minutes or until firm. Serves 4 to 6.

Sautéed Flounder in Lemon Dill Sauce

1½ tablespoons butter
1 tablespoon lemon juice
1 green onion, sliced thin
1 tablespoon chopped fresh dill
1 pound flounder fillets, cut in 4 pieces
Lemon wedges for garnish

Melt butter; add lemon juice, onion, and dill. Add flounder fillets and sauté 8 to 10 minutes. Remove fillets to serving plate, pour sauce over top and garnish with lemon wedges. Serves 4.

Flounder Cordon Bleu

6 (½-pound) flounder fillets
6 slices cooked ham
6 slices Swiss cheese
1 teaspoon grated orange rind
¼ teaspoon white pepper
6 wooden toothpicks
1 egg, beaten
1 cup unseasoned breadcrumbs
1 tablespoon butter
1 tablespoon flour
1 cup milk
¼ cup Parmesan cheese

Preheat oven to 350°. Place a slice of ham and a slice of cheese on each fillet. Sprinkle with orange rind and pepper. Roll and close with toothpicks. Dip rolled flounder in egg, cover with breadcrumbs, place in a large baking dish, and bake 20 minutes or until flesh is firm. Melt butter in a small saucepan. Stir flour into milk; add to butter and cook until thickened. Spoon sauce over flounder and cover with cheese. Serves 6.

Harold's booksigning
in Seattle.

Leave the Labor at Home
and Bid Farewell to Summer

The observance of Labor Day began over 100 years ago. On June 28, 1894, Congress passed an act making the first Monday in September a legal holiday to recognize the achievements of American workers. Labor Day also bids farewell to summer, ushers in the beginning of the school year, and is an opportunity for the final picnic of the year. At Oak Grove, we celebrate Labor Day in the afternoon, on the back gallery, with old friends, a few new guests, good food, and very little labor. No hot grill or hot kitchen. No china dishes or crystal goblets. This day is dedicated to fun, relaxation, and croquet on the front meadow. All the food and drink are prepared in advance and are served from cold platters, onto plastic plates, and cold drinks are served from the old, wooden water keg and into plastic cups.

Shrimp and Fruit Salad

1 pound (medium-sized, 36 to 40) shrimp, boiled and peeled
2 cups diced fresh apples
2 cups diced fresh pears
1 cup thinly sliced celery
2 tablespoons milk
1 tablespoon apple cider vinegar
½ cup mayonnaise
2 tablespoons grated onion
1 teaspoon salt
White pepper to taste
1 bag Spring Salad
Paprika

Cut cooked shrimp in half lengthwise and combine with apples, pears, and celery. Combine milk, vinegar, mayonnaise, onion, and salt; add shrimp mixture. Chill at least one hour and season with white pepper. Serve over salad greens. Sprinkle with paprika. Serves 6.

Harvest-Time Switchel

4 cups sugar, more or less to taste
2 cups sorghum molasses
½ cup apple cider vinegar
2 teaspoons fresh ground ginger root
2 gallons water

Mix all ingredients in a large pot with 1 quart of water; heat until dissolved. Add remaining water. Chill overnight and serve over ice. Can easily be halved.

Broiled Cold Venison Loin

½ venison loin
10 ounces teriyaki sauce
Cooking oil
Salt and pepper

Soak loin 1 hour in teriyaki sauce. Coat with cooking oil, and sprinkle with salt and pepper to taste. Roast in 350° oven until internal temperature is 138°. Coat with additional oil as needed. Remove, roll in aluminum foil and allow to rest in refrigerator until chilled. Slice thin and serve cold.

Labor Day at Oak Grove.

Seafood Dip

3 cans cooked shrimp or crab
16 ounces sour cream
1 (8-ounce) package cream cheese, softened
1 cup minced celery
1 cup minced onion
Dash Worcestershire sauce
2 lemons, juiced
Thin crackers
Cayenne pepper

Combine shrimp or crab and sour cream. Mix in cream cheese, celery, onion, Worcestershire, and lemon juice; chill 2 hours. Spread on crackers and lightly dust with cayenne.

Peach Sorbet

1 cup water
½ cup sugar
8 small peaches, peeled and cored
Juice of 1 lemon
1 tablespoon peach brandy, optional
1 cup fresh raspberries or blackberries
Mint sprigs

Mix together water and sugar in a stainless steel or ceramic sauce pan and bring to a boil. Simmer 5 minutes. Remove cover, and set aside to cool. Purée or process peaches to make 1 cup pulp. Combine all ingredients and process in an ice cream machine. Serve in chilled wine glasses and garnish with fresh berries and a mint sprig. Serves 6.

Fall

It's too Hot to Hunt Wild Geese

Wild geese have created a problem for themselves and have given many of us a grand opportunity. The general goose population has dramatically increased and permanent resident populations have established themselves along the flyways. The grand opportunity that I speak of is the September Nuisance Goose Season. Each September my old friend Jim surprises me with an early morning call advising me that he will be stopping by Oak Grove in a few hours with some geese. I am never ungrateful when friends offer me a portion of their harvest. However, these September geese always arrive hot and in full feather. It did not take me long to realize that hand-plucking a brace of geese on a hot September day was not my calling. I quickly learned how to remove the breasts and the liver. Which brings me to my point: the breasts, when gently cooked to rare or no more than medium rare, offer world-class culinary possibilities.

Goose and Oyster Gumbo

½ cup flour
½ cup cooking oil
1 green bell pepper, chopped
½ cup chopped celery
3 onions, chopped
3 quarts water
2 goose breasts, cubed
Salt and pepper
1 pint oysters and liquid
⅓ cup chopped parsley
Tabasco sauce

Brown flour in oil until dark; stirring constantly. Add bell pepper, celery and onion; cook until just soft. Remove to a large pot; add water, goose, and salt and pepper to taste. Simmer 2 hours. Add oysters with liquid, parsley, and Tabasco to taste; simmer another 10 minutes. Serves 6 to 8.

Wild Goose Cheese Burgers

1 goose breast, cubed
½ teaspoon black pepper, divided
5 tablespoons Italian dressing
½ teaspoon seasoned salt
¼ teaspoon garlic powder
1 cup flour
Cooking oil
1 tablespoon butter
2 large onions, chopped
1 (8-ounce) can mushroom pieces
8 hamburger buns
8 mozzarella cheese slices

Mix together goose, ¼ teaspoon pepper, and salad dressing. Grind with a fine blade. Refrigerate 2 hours. Mix together ¼ teaspoon pepper, seasoned salt, garlic powder, and flour. Form ground goose into patties and coat with flour mixture. Heat oil and fry patties to medium. In a separate skillet, melt butter and sauté onions until just clear. Add mushroom pieces and sauté until warm. Toast buns, add burgers and top with onion mixture and cheese slice. Serves 4 to 8.

Cajun Crockpot Wild Goose

2 goose fillets, cubed
1 medium onion, chopped
4 celery stalks, chopped
1 pound fresh mushrooms
4 jalapeño peppers, chopped (optional)
¾ cup milk
1 can cream of mushroom soup
1 tablespoon salt
1 teaspoon pepper
⅓ cup flour
½ cup water

Place all ingredients, except flour and water, in a crockpot. Cook 8 hours on low heat. Mix flour into cold water, stir into crockpot and cook 30 minutes. Serve over rice. Serves 4.

Goose Breasts with Apricots

1 (10- to 12-ounce) can apricots
1 tablespoon grated orange rind
10 tablespoons (1 stick plus 2 tablespoons) butter, divided
2 cups red wine
¼ teaspoon pepper
1 goose breast

Drain apricots, purée or press through a food mill. Place in a saucepan with orange rind, 2 tablespoons butter, wine and pepper. Bring to a boil; reduce heat and continue to cook until reduced by ⅓. Set aside. Slice breast into two layers and sauté in 8 tablespoons butter until medium or 138° on a meat thermometer. Allow to rest 10 minutes. Slice breasts very thin and cover with apricot sauce. Serves 4.

Oysters Yes. "R" Month, Maybe.

Americans eat more oysters than anyone else in the world. At one time the concern about eating oysters harvested only in months which have an "R" had a measure of validity. It did not have anything to do with an "R" month. It had a great deal to do with the weather in which the seafood was shipped. "R" months are the cooler months of the year: September thru April. However, oysters which are harvested in the "R" months are generally larger and more flavorful. Before the advent of mobile cooling systems, commercial transporters had to rely on ice to keep seafood fresh. If the weather turned unseasonably hot or there were delays in route, the ice could melt and the seafood would spoil in a very short time. Today there is no reason to be concerned. Modern refrigerated land and air transports ship fresh seafood around the world in a matter of hours. Without even thinking about it, we can feast today on Fillet of Sole (flounder) that was swimming in the North Sea off Scotland last night and Oysters on the Half Shell that were on the bottom of the Gulf of Mexico this morning.

Cream of Oyster Stew

1 pint oysters
4 tablespoons butter
½ cup chopped celery
½ cup chopped onion
½ cup diced carrots
¼ teaspoon white pepper
1 can cream of mushroom soup
½ cup milk
¼ cup parsley, chopped
Sherry (optional)

Drain oysters, saving liquid. Melt butter in a saucepan and sauté celery, onion, and carrots 5 minutes. Add pepper and oyster liquid. Add mushroom soup and milk; stir until smooth. Heat to low simmer; add parsley and oysters. Heat until oysters are plump and the edges begin to ruffle. Serve immediately. A splash of sherry can be added to each serving. Serves 4.

Grilled Whole Oyster Appetizers with Lemon, Wine and Butter Sauce

2 dozen oysters, in shell
Juice of 4 lemons or 3 lemons and one lime
White wine
1 cup real butter, melted
4 tablespoons minced fresh parsley
4 tablespoons minced fresh basil

Preheat grill. Scrub the outside of oysters and discard those that are already open. Whisk together remaining ingredients and set aside. Place oysters on grill until shells open (approximately 5 minutes). Lift off top shell. Return oysters to grill. Re-whisk lemon and butter sauce and spoon over oysters. Grill another 4 to 5 minutes. Plate and serve. Serves 4.

Fried Oysters

1 pint oysters, drained
2 cups dry pancake mix
Oil for deep frying
Salt
Cocktail or tartar sauce

Preheat oil to 350°. Toss a few oysters at a time in the pancake mix until well coated; shake off excess mix. Deep fry small batches until golden brown, 1½ to 2 minutes. Drain, lightly salt, and serve with cocktail or tartar sauce. Serves 4.

Spring Salad with Poppy Seed Dressing

1 cup salad oil
½ teaspoon grated lemon rind
Juice of 2 lemons
¼ cup white vinegar
1½ teaspoons onion juice (scrape onion)
½ teaspoon salt
¾ cup sugar
1 teaspoon dry mustard
1¼ tablespoons poppy seeds
1 bag prepared spring salad mix

Place all ingredients, except salad mix, in a quart jar and shake until mixed well. Refrigerate until chilled. Pour over salad mix. Serves 6 to 8.

Poochie was a Feist Dog

Poochie was my first dog. I suspect it was my grandfather who brought Poochie home as he was fond of rescuing stray animals. At different times, he brought home a pet raccoon, a pet bobcat, two baby alligators, a horned toad from Texas, an opossum, and a de-scented skunk (just for me) from Arkansas. It was Poochie that I remember best; because Poochie was a Feist dog. Everyone knows that Feist dogs are natural-born squirrel hunters. In the fall, Dad would take Poochie and me down to the hardwood bottoms in search of gray squirrels. Poochie was in her element. She instinctively and intuitively knew what to do. Many of those memories are now blurred with the passage of years, but I can remember Poochie dashing off and listening to her little popping bark. Dad would lift me up, sit me down on a stump and tell me to listen. It wasn't long before we would hear Poochie's bark change to a rapid-fire squeal/bark. Dad would stand me up and say, "Let's go. Poochies got another one treed." We would find Poochie bouncing up and down and around the tree. Dad taught me how you need two people (or a Feist dog) to see a tight-sitting squirrel. He would walk around the tree and the squirrel would come around to my side. When I became older, Poochie and I would hunt together and she would move the squirrels around the tree for me. One of these days I am going to find another Feist dog and I do not think that I should name her Poochie—there was only one Poochie.

Braised Squirrel

4 tablespoons cooking oil
½ cup flour
½ teaspoon seasoned salt
¼ teaspoon pepper
2 squirrels, serving-size pieces
½ cup water
1 onion, coarsely chopped
3 carrots, sliced

Heat stew pot; add oil. Place flour, salt, and pepper in a paper bag. Add squirrel a few pieces at a time and shake well. Fry squirrel until brown; reduce heat, add water, onions, and carrots. Cover and cook on low heat 40 to 50 minutes. Stir bottom to prevent sticking. Serves 4.

Squirrel Mulligan Stew

1 cup flour
Salt and pepper
3 to 4 pounds squirrel, cut into pieces
1 tablespoon butter
2 quarts chicken broth
1 tablespoon cooking oil
2 cups English peas
1 large onion, coarsely chopped
2 large potatoes, 1-inch squares
4 carrots, ½-inch squares
2 cans tomato sauce
2 cloves garlic, minced
2 bay leaves
1 tablespoon dried thyme
2 tablespoons chili powder
4 tomatoes, peeled and quartered

Mix flour, salt and pepper; coat squirrel pieces and brown in butter. Gently remove meat from bones. Bring broth to a boil. Place squirrel and remaining ingredients (except tomatoes) in broth; cover and simmer 1 hour over low heat. Stir to keep from sticking. Add tomatoes and simmer another hour.

Squirrel Jambalaya

1 squirrel, serving-size pieces
salt and cayenne pepper, to taste
3 tablespoons cooking oil
¼ green bell pepper, chopped
3 stalks celery, finely chopped
4 tablespoons minced parsley
1 garlic clove, minced
1 large white onion, coarsely chopped
1½ cups water
2 cups long grain rice

Season squirrel with salt and cayenne; brown in oil. Remove and gently sauté bell pepper, celery, parsley, garlic, and onion. Return squirrel, cover and cook 20 minutes over low heat. Stir in water, salt to taste, and rice. Cook 30 minutes over low heat or until rice is cooked. Serves 2 to 4.

Dorado, Mahi Mahi, Dolphin:
The Same in any Skin

Dorado are one of the most beautiful fish in the sea. When seen swimming, you are immediately awestruck with the iridescent glowing of pure gold, vivid green, bright yellows, and shades of turquoise blues. Four things I know for sure about dorado are: they respond to chum slicks, are willing to eat a variety of lures and flies, the school will follow the first hooked fish up to the boat, and they are delicious to eat. Whether you fish the deep blue waters of the Pacific, the Gulf of Mexico, or up the eastern seaboard, you will find dorado. Each one you catch is as exciting as the last and each catch is a joy to the eyes, a challenge to the muscles, and a story worth the re-telling. When first hooked, the dorado explodes from the water with a burst of foam and a blast of color followed by line screaming off the reel. When the first fish begins to tire, just let him swim around because the remaining school is likely to follow and then the real fun begins.

Sautéed Dorado with Tomato and Basil

1 tablespoon cooking oil
1 pound dorado fillets
1 tablespoon minced garlic
⅓ cup sliced red onions
⅔ cup chicken broth
2 tablespoons nuoc nam (fish sauce) or teriyaki
1 tablespoon rice wine vinegar or lemon juice
1 tablespoon sugar
¼ cup diced white onion
2 tablespoons tomato paste
½ cup chopped fresh basil
2 ½ cups, cubed tomatoes

Heat 1 tablespoon cooking oil in a sauté pan and fry fillets until flesh just begins to firm; remove and cover. Sauté garlic and red onions in the same pan. Stir in chicken broth, fish sauce, vinegar, sugar, onion, tomato paste, and simmer until thickened. Remove sauce from stove and stir in basil. Place dorado on serving plates, spoon sauce over and sprinkle with tomato cubes. Serves 4.

Hawaiian Mahi-Mahi

1½ pounds mahi-mahi fillets
Salt and pepper
1 cup whole salted macadamia nuts, divided
1 cup unsweetened coconut milk

Preheat oven to 350°. Cut fish into 4 (1-inch wide) pieces and place on bottom of a 12 ½x8 ½-inch baking dish and sprinkle with salt and pepper. Sprinkle with ½ macadamia nuts and pour coconut milk around fillets. Bake 18 minutes or until flesh is firm. Chop remaining nuts and sprinkle over fillets. Serves 4.

Dolphin Amandine

4 dolphin fillets
Salt and pepper
½ cup cooking oil
Juice of ½ lemon
1 garlic clove, very finely minced
¼ cup slivered almonds
2 tablespoons real butter
Minced parsley
¼ teaspoon lemon or lime juice

Sprinkle fillets with salt and pepper to taste; marinate 30 minutes in refrigerator in oil, lemon juice and garlic. Grill 5 minues on each side until flesh is firm brushing with marinade while cooking. Sauté almonds in butter until brown; mix in parsley and lemon juice. Spoon over fish. Serves 4.

Baked Dorado
in White Wine and Mustard Sauce

1 cup Dijon mustard
1 cup mayonnaise
1 cup dry white wine
6 dorado fillets, serving-size pieces
Butter
¼ cup minced parsley

Mix mustard, mayonnaise and wine. Place fillets in a large buttered casserole dish, cover with sauce, and bake 20 minutes at 300° until flesh is firm. Remove to serving plates and sprinkle with parsley. Serves 6.

Gourmet Dining in a Small and Speedy Package

I know of no one who has eaten their measure of wild duck that will disagree that the diminutive little teal is one of the best, if not the best, eating of all the species of wild duck. With a Mallard weighing in at 2 ¼ pounds, the little 8 to 16 ounce teal is no culinary lightweight. Flying at 57 miles per hour, teal are one of the faster flying ducks. Their speed, coupled with their small size, make them appear farther away than they are and they seem to fly even faster. If you are accustomed to hunting geese or larger duck, a fast-flying teal will be on top of you before you can raise your shotgun. In addition to their speed and small size they fly in very erratic patterns with the flock flying in unison. Teal are usually one of the first ducks to migrate south, which accounts for many southern states having a September Teal-Only hunting season. Cooking teal is more similar to cooking quail, cornish hen, and dove than they are to cooking duck. Cook them very gently and watch carefully that you do not over-cook the small birds. Teal and other duck are best cooked rare or no more than medium rare.

Sauerkraut Stuffed Teal

4 whole teal
Pepper
¼ cup brown sugar
2 cups sauerkraut

Preheat oven to 500°. Dust inside of birds with pepper. Mix sugar into sauerkraut, stuff birds, wrap in heavy foil and set in a baking pan. Cook 10 minutes; lower temperature to 300° and cook 2 hours. Remove; turn bird over to rest 2 minutes before serving. Serves 2 to 4.

Gingered Breast of Teal

¼ cup fresh orange juice
1 teaspoon soy sauce
¼ cup cane syrup
2 teaspoons white pepper
8 teal breasts
4 tablespoons real butter, divided
2 tablespoons sesame oil
1 cup chicken broth
1 tablespoon grated orange rind
1 (2-inch) piece ginger, peeled and julienned
1 tablespoon chopped garlic
½ cup sliced green onions with tops
Salt to taste

Combine orange juice, soy sauce, syrup, and pepper; add breasts. Let sit at room temperature for two hours, stirring every 15 minutes. Melt 2 tablespoons butter and sesame oil in a skillet. Gently sauté breasts (reserve marinade) 2 to 3 minutes on each side until center is rare; remove and keep warm. Stir in marinade and remaining ingredients except remaining butter and salt. Bring to a boil, lower to simmer and reduce to ½ original volume. Add remaining butter. Return breasts and heat several minutes on both sides. Salt to taste. Slice breasts. Strain sauce and pour over breasts. Serves 2 to 4.

Broiled Lemon Teal

4 whole teal, split in half
Salt and pepper
3 tablespoons unsalted real butter
2 tablespoons fresh lemon juice
1 tablespoon sugar

Season teal with salt and pepper. Combine remaining ingredients. Marinate 30 minutes in refrigerator. Place on broiler rack and cook 10 minutes per side, basting often. While teal is cooking, bring marinade to a boil on stovetop; lower heat to simmer until teal is cooked. Place teal on serving plate and cover with marinade. Serves 2 to 4.

Le Canard d'Orange

1 package wild rice mix plus ingredients to prepare per directions
½ pound unsalted real butter
1 jar orange marmalade
Salt and pepper
4 whole teal, split in half

Prepare wild rice according to dirctions on package; cover and set aside. Melt butter, stir in marmalade, and set aside. Salt and pepper teal halves to taste. Heat grill and lay skin down; cooking until brown. Turn and cook until brown and flesh is just firm. Baste frequently with marmalade sauce and spoon on a little when served. Plate teal with wild rice on the side. Serves 2 to 4.

Wild Goose: The Trick is in the Cooking

The trick is in the cooking, but the quality is in the harvest. Wild geese vary from domestic geese in that domestic geese are fed a consistently nutritious diet, do not have to exert themselves and are harvested while they are young. Wild geese have to work for their food and we have very little control over the age of our harvest. There is no getting around it, old geese are just tough and are best chopped and cooked in long simmering stews and gumbos. It may be possible to salvage breasts, but don't even think about roasting an old wild goose. Aging geese is difficult at best and impossible on the wing, but there are two things that may help. Hold the goose by the bill and if the bill bends or breaks under the weight of the goose then the goose is probably young. The tips of the wing feathers of an old goose may appear ragged while the wing tips on a young goose may be smooth and sharp.

Baked Goose with Currant Sauce

1 (6- to 8-pound) young wild goose
1 quart buttermilk
2 apples, sliced
1 cup pitted prunes
5 slices bacon
3 sticks (1½ cups) real butter, melted
¼ cup flour
¾ cup chicken broth
1 cup sour cream
4 tablespoons red currant jelly

Place goose in buttermilk and refrigerate 8 hours. Remove goose, rinse and wipe dry. Preheat oven to 325°. Stuff with apples and prunes. Truss goose with cotton twine. Place bacon on goose; tightly wrap in foil. Bake 3 hours or until tender. Remove foil and baste with 2 sticks melted butter until brown. Melt 1 stick butter in a saucepan, whisk flour into broth and stir into butter. Prior to serving, stir in sour cream and jelly. Remove stuffing and arrange around goose. Serve with sauce. Serves 4.

Baked Goose Casserole

4 cups dried white navy beans
4 tomatoes, peeled, seeded and cubed
4 large white onions, chopped
¼ pound Italian salami, cubed
4 whole peppercorns
2 teaspoons minced parsley
¼ teaspoon dried rosemary
2 garlic cloves, minced
1 bay leaf, halved
1 (6- to 8-pound) wild goose, serving-size pieces
Salt and pepper
½ cup olive oil
3 cups white wine, divided
6 garlic flavored or other sausages
1 cup unseasoned breadcrumbs

Place beans in water, cover and soak overnight. Drain and discard beans that float. Preheat oven to 225°. Place beans in a large covered casserole dish and mix in tomatoes, onions, salami, peppercorns, parsley, rosemary, cloves and bay leaf. Cover and bake 6 hours. Rub goose with salt and pepper and brown in oil. Reduce heat, add wine, cover and simmer 30 minutes. Add goose and sauce to casserole. Sauté sausage; reserve fat and add sausage to goose. Cover and bake at 250° 1½ hours. Brown breadcrumbs in fat and sprinkle over casserole. Bake 10 minutes uncovered. Serves 14.

Oriental Sautéed Goose Breasts

2 wild goose breasts
2 (8-ounce) cans sliced mushrooms
3 medium white onions, chopped
1 (2-ounce) package slivered almonds
Salt and pepper
2 packages Oriental Rice-A-Roni
3 celery stalks, 1-inch-long pieces
1 each red and green bell pepper, cut in strips

Parboil goose 20 minutes. Cut into 1-inch cubes and reserve water. Place goose, mushrooms, onions, and almonds in a sauté pan and cook 15 minutes. Season to taste with salt and pepper. Using reserved water, cook Rice-A-Roni per directions; add celery and bell peppers when ½ cooked. When rice is done, combine with goose breast pieces and serve. Serves 4.

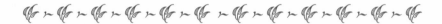

Broach was a Hermit man and one Fine Coon Hunter

Broach lived in a one-room shack on a small rise in the field and a fair walk from his brother's house. The walls were covered with peeling newspapers; there was an old mattress on the floor for sleeping. Piles of old magazines were scattered about and a wood burning stove/heater was in the corner. I was very young at the time and the questions I asked were not the ones I would ask today. Broach was known to be the best coon hunter in all of Lauderdale County. When my grandfather would take me with him to visit Broach's brother, I would persist until I was allowed to walk out and visit with Broach. There was something mysterious and exciting about the thought of walking through the woods at night and listening to the hounds when they treed a coon. After several years of sitting and listening to Broach as he talked about his "night adventures," I finally persuaded him to take my grandfather and me coon hunting. My night was spent wet up to my waist in creek water, falling over logs and getting caught in invisible brier patches. To top it off, I finally fell and broke the glass in my Coleman lantern. We "think" we treed one coon. After that night, I lost interest in coon hunting—expectations and reality were farther apart than I had imagined.

Baked Raccoon Casserole

1 (4- to 6-pound) raccoon
Salt and pepper
1 large yellow onion, chopped
2 garlic cloves, minced
3 carrots, sliced
2 large potatoes, chunked
Tomato juice to cover

Cut raccoon into serving-size pieces. Place in a large pot and cover with water; season then slow boil until tender. Remove meat and place in a casserole dish. Add remaining ingredients. Bake at 325° 1 hour or until vegetables are done. Serves 4.

Sweet Potato Stuffed Raccoon

1 pound baked sweet potatoes, peeled and mashed
½ cup raisins or sultanas
½ cup unseasoned breadcrumbs
1 to 4 apples, peeled, cored and chopped
1 cup butter, melted
2 tablespoons lemon juice
¼ cup brown sugar, packed
½ teaspoon ground cinnamon
⅛ teaspoon ground ginger
Salt and pepper
1 (4- to 6-pound) raccoon

Preheat oven to 325°. Mix together first 9 ingredients to make stuffing. Salt and pepper inside of body, gently stuff with potato mixture and sew shut. Bake 3 to 4 hours. When half done, turn over. Serves 4 to 6.

Raccoon Stew

1 raccoon, quartered
4 carrots, chopped
1 large onion, chopped
3 potatoes, cubed
2 stalks celery, chopped
1 (16-ounce) can stewed tomatoes
¼ teaspoon dried basil
Salt and pepper
Cooked rice for 6

Parboil raccoon until tender; skim surface foam as needed. Remove meat from bones and mix with remaining ingredients (except rice) in a stew pot. Simmer on low until vegetables are tender. If stew needs thickening, mix 1 tablespoon flour with 2 tablespoons water and stir into simmering stew a small bit at a time until thickened. Serves 6.

Grilled Raccoon

1 cup ketchup
1½ cups melted butter or cooking oil
¼ cup brown sugar, packed
1 tablespoon Worcestershire sauce
1 tablespoon garlic powder or to taste
1 tablespoon onion powder or to taste
1 tablespoon salt
¼ cup lemon juice
1 teaspoon black pepper
1 (4- to 6-pound) raccoon

Make grilling sauce by combining all ingredients except raccoon. Cut raccoon into pieces and simmer in salted water until tender. Soak in sauce for 30 minutes, grill and baste with sauce. Serves 4.

Venison Sausage the Easy Way

Amaze your friends and astound your family with your sausage making skills. Sausage making is not difficult. You can make outstanding sausage in your own kitchen. It is a little messy and cleanliness is next to godliness. Stick with making patty sausage and leave the links to the professionals. Make your sausage in small batches. Rytek Kutas, the recognized master of sausage making, says that it is perfectly all right to thaw frozen venison and then re-freeze it as finished sausage. The only specialized tools that you need are a hand-cranked food grinder, a roll of plastic wrap, and string. When my ol' friend Jim calls and wants to know if I will help him make some venison sausage "today" I start mumbling something about the weather making my arthritis ache and my trick knee is acting up again. Since ol' Jim is one of my best friends, I really wanted to work up several breakfast sausage recipes that he could easily make in his kitchen. Take your time, plan your work, and have fun. Invite the kids to work with you and let them get elbow-deep in sausage.

Baked Apples filled with Venison Sausage

3 large tart apples
1 cup Hunter's Venison Sausage Patties (see recipe page 124)
1 teaspoon salt
2 tablespoons brown sugar

Preheat oven to 375°. Cut a slice from the tops of the apples. Scoop out the cores and pulp, leaving sides ¾-inch thick. Cut the pulp from the cores and chop it. Combine chopped apple with sausage. Sprinkle apples with salt and brown sugar. Fill the apples heaping full with the sausage/apple mixture. Bake at 350° until sausage is done and apples are tender. To serve, slice apples in half. Serves 6.

Baked Venison Sausage Ring

¼ cup crushed cornflakes
1 pound Hot Italian Venison Sausage (see recipe page 125)
1 tablespoon minced white onion
¾ cup unseasoned breadcrumbs
2 tablespoons chopped parsley
9 eggs, divided
Butter
Chopped parsley and paprika for garnish

Preheat oven to 350°. Lightly grease a 7-inch ring mold. Cover bottom with cornflakes. Combine sausage, onion, breadcrumbs, parsley, and 1 beaten egg. Place in mold and bake 15 minutes. Drain fat and bake another 15 minutes or until done. Scramble remaining eggs in skillet in butter. Invert ring onto a hot platter and fill the center with scrambled eggs. Garnish with chopped parsley and paprika. Serves 2 to 4.

Hunter's Venison Sausage Patties

2 tablespoons salt
2 teaspoons black pepper
¾ teaspoon mace
¼ teaspoon ground nutmeg
¼ teaspoon ground cloves
½ teaspoon ground allspice
½ teaspoon garlic powder
4 pounds venison, cubed
4 pounds boneless pork butt, cubed

Combine seasonings and mix well with meats. Grind twice with a fine grinding disc. Measure out ⅓ cups of the mixture and shape into patties. Place a piece of waxed paper on BOTH sides of each patty, stack and wrap with aluminum foil, freeze or refrigerate no more than three days. To serve, fry patties.

Hot Italian Venison Sausage

6 pounds venison, cubed
2 pounds boneless pork butt, cubed
1½ pounds bacon
2 teaspoons salt
1 teaspoon black pepper
4 teaspoons fennel seeds
4 teaspoons garlic powder
1 teaspoon cayenne pepper or to taste
1 teaspoon red pepper flakes
Plastic wrap
String

Mix meats together. Mix spices and sprinkle over meats. Toss until well mixed. Grind twice with a fine grinding disc. Place on a sheet of plastic wrap, shape sausage into 1-inch round logs and wrap 4 times with plastic. Twist one end of the plastic shut and tie with string. Work out air pockets, twist off other end and tie with string. Store in refrigerator for no longer than three days. To serve, slice and fry.

Hot Italian Venison Sausage.

Bow Season: Best Deer Hunt of the Year

When September gets close, I always get a case of bow hunting fever. It is then that I spend my Tuesday and Thursday mornings at Bill's Archery seeing what toll another year of age has taken on my body. During one recent practice session, I sat resting between rounds when I met Johnny. Johnny was maybe ten or twelve. He walked in with the confidence of a seasoned veteran, his little compound bow and a handful of inexpensive chrome tipped plastic arrows. Johnny asked if it was all right for him to shoot a while. As I sat and watched, it became apparent that his little bow was nowhere close to being zeroed, and I could see his frustration starting to show. I eased out and asked Bill, "What size group could one reasonably expect to shoot with that bow?" "If he can consistently hit a small paper plate at twenty yards, he will be shooting about as good as the bow." I asked Johnny if he had ever zeroed his bow and he replied, "What is that?" I hung my bow on the wall and for the next half hour we talked. We talked about why a bow shoots like it does, the difference between where you want the arrow to go versus where the sight pin actually was when the arrow released... and about being honest with oneself. When it came time for Johnny to leave, he was shooting eight-inch groups and looking forward to the opening of bow season. As I was leaving, Bill said, "He will do just fine. Johnny has only had his bow for a week and that was the first time he had shot it." As for me, I was glad that I had hung up my bow and taken the time to talk. I remembered how someone had once taken the time with me. Johnny will do just fine.

Garlic Venison Sausage Patties

2 pounds boneless venison, chopped
¾ pound boneless pork chops, chopped
1 small white onion, chopped
4 garlic cloves, minced
2 teaspoons salt
1 teaspoon black pepper
1 teaspoon ground sage (optional)
½ teaspoon ground thyme
¼ teaspoon ground nutmeg
¼ teaspoon ground ginger
⅛ teaspoon ground allspice

Mix all ingredients and grind once with a coarse grinding disc. Mix well and grind again with a fine grinding disc. Shape into patties or use plastic wrap and roll into a large roll and refrigerate overnight. Store in the refrigerator for up to 3 days or package and freeze. Makes 2 ¾ pounds.

Venison Steak Italian Style

4 (1- to 1¼-inch-thick) venison steaks
Flour
½ onion, sliced
2 tablespoons cooking oil
1 green bell pepper, cut into strips
1 can Italian tomatoes with liquid
Dash garlic powder
Dash ground oregano
Salt and pepper to taste

Dredge venison steaks in flour. Fry steaks and onions in oil until brown. Add remaining ingredients, cover and simmer ½ to 1 hour. Serves 2 to 4.

Venison Chili

3 pounds ground venison
4 green bell peppers, chopped
5 garlic cloves, minced
6 large onions, chopped
2 tablespoons cooking oil
1 to 2 teaspoons Tabasco sauce
2 cans tomato sauce
2 tablespoons chili powder
1 tablespoon cumin
1 teaspoon cayenne pepper
1 teaspoon salt
5 chili peppers, minced (optional)
1 can red kidney beans with liquid
Cooked rice for 4 to 6
Shredded sharp Cheddar cheese

Brown venison, bell peppers, garlic and onions in deep skillet with oil. Add Tabasco, tomato sauce, and spices; simmer 45 minutes. Add chili peppers and beans; simmer 15 minutes more. Serve over rice and sprinkle with cheese. Serves 4 to 6.

Potato and Carrot Crockpot Venison Roast

1 small rolled venison sirloin roast
3 medium onions, whole, halved, sliced or chopped
8 small potatoes, whole, halved or quartered
2 medium carrots, halved, quartered or sliced
1 garlic clove, whole, sliced or chopped
1¾ to 2 cups French onion soup
Salt and pepper

Place venison roast, onions, potatoes, carrots, and garlic in a crockpot. Pour in soup stock and season to taste with salt and pepper. Set crockpot on low and cook 8 hours. Serves 4 to 6.

My Deer Ain't Tough and My Deer Don't Stink

There are many people who are averse to eating venison because their first dining experience was less than satisfying. I was once a member of that group. How many times have I heard people say, "Venison is tough and smells gamey!" They are correct, and at the same time they are very wrong. Some venison is tough and some venison smells gamey. The toughness is the function of age and the strong smell is the function of the natural chemicals that build up in the tissues of a frightened and tired animal or male animals with high levels of seasonal hormones. An old cow will be tough and if you chase a pig around the pen before slaughter, it will taste gamey. The keys to harvesting venison that is always tender and sweet smelling is to harvest young/mature deer at a time when they are rested and are dispatched instantly. Do not harvest male animals in the time of the year when they have high levels of seasonal hormones. With the high population of deer we have today, there is no reason that a hunter cannot do selective harvesting and have the patience to wait until a calm deer is in position for a clean and instant harvest. I prefer to harvest my bucks early in the season and harvest does later in the year.

Harold processing venison in his skinning shed.

Venison Summer Sausage

5 pounds venison burger
6 teaspoons pickling salt
2 ½ teaspoons mustard seed
2 ½ teaspoons coarse ground pepper
3 garlic cloves, minced
1 teaspoon hickory smoke salt

Combine all ingredients, cover and refrigerate 24 hours. Mix again and refrigerate 24 hours. Shape into 5 logs, place in an oven proof dish and bake 8 hours at 165°. Turn every two hours. Can be stored in refrigerator for up to 3 days or packaged and frozen.

Venison Chops in Sour Cream

½ teaspoon ground sage
½ teaspoon salt
Dash white or black pepper
6 venison chops, ¾-inch thick
2 tablespoons shortening
2 medium onions, sliced
1 beef bouillon cube
¼ cup boiling water
½ cup sour cream
1 tablespoon flour
1 tablespoon crushed parsley flakes

Rub sage, salt and pepper into chops. Heat shortening and brown chops on both sides. Pour off grease and add onions to chops. Dissolve bouillon cube in boiling water and add to pan. Cover and simmer 30 minutes or until chops are tender. Place chops on platter. Mix sour cream and flour and slowly stir into pan drippings; simmer until mixture begins to boil. If needed, add water to thin and pour over chops. Sprinkle with parsley. Serves 3 to 4.

Venison Steaks with Apricot-Plum Sauce

½ cup apricot preserves
1 cup plum preserves
½ cup applesauce
2 tablespoons honey
⅓ cup apple cider vinegar
3 drops garlic juice
6 venison steaks, ½- to ¾-inch thick
Cooked rice for 6

Combine all ingredients, except venison and rice, in a saucepan and bring to boil. Reduce heat to medium and cook 5 minutes, stirring frequently. Remove sauce from stove and set aside. Place steaks on bottom of a greased broiler pan, cover with ½ cup sauce and cook until just beginning to brown. Turn steaks, cover with ½ cup sauce and cook until just beginning to brown. Serve with remaining sauce and rice. Serves 6.

Jerky, Jerky

I suspect that some form of jerky has been around almost as long as man. There is no record of when jerky was first made, but I can picture a Neanderthal butchering game on a hot day then coming back several months later to find that the remnants of meat had dried on the hot rocks and were edible. Jerky is nothing more than raw meat with most of its water removed. It is not cooked. It is this dehydration that preserves it and prevents it from spoiling. Most modern jerky recipes call for a salt-based marinade that acts as a pickling agent and departs flavor. A 10-pound venison hindquarter will yield five pounds meat after bones, fat, and white connective tissue has been removed. This five pounds of meat will lose 60% of its weight during the dehydration process — leaving two pounds of finished jerky. You can make jerky by hanging it in a hot summer attic for several days or you can purchase a dehydrator. You may wish to use your stove; a gas stove is preferable to an electric one. Fit oven racks with a ½x½-inch screen and make a bottom drip tray out of heavy aluminum foil. Lay meat on racks without overlapping. Set the thermostat on the lowest setting 130° to 150° and leave a small gap in the door. Check for dryness at about five hours and remove pieces as they become leather-hard. Store jerky in a freezer until ready to eat.

Creamed Venison

1 cup venison jerky, ⅛- to ¼-inch pieces
½ cup hot water
2 tablespoons real butter
1 tablespoon all-purpose flour
1 cup milk
½ teaspoon pepper
Salt to taste

Soak jerky in hot water for 20 minutes and then return to a slow boil for 5 minutes. Drain, and set aside. Melt butter in a skillet, stir in flour and slightly brown. Stir in milk and cook until gravy is thickened. Add jerky, pepper, and salt to taste. Serve over biscuits.

Hot and Spicy Jerky

For mild jerky, leave out the hot spices.

5 pounds red venison meat, slice ¼-inch across the grain
1 cup teriyaki sauce
1 cup water
½ teaspoon Tabasco sauce
¼ teaspoon liquid smoke
8 tablespoons lemon pepper
2 teaspoons cayenne pepper
1 tablespoon crushed red pepper
½ teaspoon garlic powder
2 tablespoons coarse black pepper
1½ cups dark brown sugar

Mix all ingredients and refrigerate 24 hours. Stir and rotate venison 6 or more times during the 24-hour period. Dehydrate until leather hard. Seal jerky in small plastic bags and freeze until needed.

Buttermilk Biscuits

2 ½ cups all-purpose flour
1 teaspoon salt
4 teaspoons baking powder
3 tablespoons vegetable shortening
1 cup buttermilk, as needed

Preheat oven to 500°. Combine flour, salt, and baking powder; cut in vegetable shortening. Add just enough buttermilk to make sticky dough. Knead for no more than 30 seconds. Roll out to ½-inch thickness and cut with biscuit cutter. Place on a greased baking sheet and bake 10 minutes or until golden.

Baked Cheese Grits

¾ cup quick grits
1 egg, beaten
3 cups water
1 cup shredded Cheddar cheese
2 tablespoons butter
Dash cayenne pepper, to taste

Cook grits according to directions on package. Preheat oven to 350°. Grease a 1½-quart baking dish. Mix a small amount of cooked grits into beaten egg and stir back into remaining grits. Add remaining ingredients and cook over low heat until cheese is melted. Pour into baking dish and bake 30 to 40 minutes or until top is set. Let stand 5 minutes before serving.

Cork Popping for Fall Specks

As the water begins to cool, speckled trout fishing along the coastlines will begin to heat up. The simplest and most popular tackle for speckled trout fishing is the Popping Cork Technique/Rig. The best results are obtained by popping the cork periodically to simulate live action. By varying the retrieve, frequency of popping, and the depth of bait, the best action for catching trout can be found. Local bait and tackle shops can give you advice as to what rigs are working best in their area. Hook live shrimp from the tail forward. Smaller bait-fish such as mullet can also be used. As the water cools, the specks begin to seek out deeper bay water such as ship canals and passes. Look for feeding gulls, as trout will chase shrimp and small fish to the surface. Oil slicks are also good indicators as the feeding and excited trout cause oil to be released from their bait-fish. Cast into the center of the gulls or the slick and do not be surprised when you get an immediate strike. Most of the trout you land will be in the 2 to 3 pound range. These are the perfect size for filleting, broiling, stuffing and baking; cut larger fish into steaks. Clean and place your catch on ice as rapidly as possible as the delicate meat loses quality quickly if not chilled.

Grilled Speckled Trout

Corn oil
4 speckled trout fillets
Flour
Salt, pepper, and Tabasco sauce

Heat grill to medium and brush with corn oil. Wash fillets; pat dry. Make a medium-thick paste with flour and corn oil. Season with salt, pepper and Tabasco sauce to taste. Coat trout with the paste and grill 6 to 8 minutes or until flesh is firm. Turn only once. Serve with Turnips in White Sauce. Serves 4.

Turnips in White Sauce

8 small turnips, pared and diced
2 cups milk
4 tablespoons flour
4 tablespoons butter, melted
Salt and pepper

Cook turnips until tender; season to taste. Whisk together flour and milk; add butter. Cook over low heat, stirring constantly, until thickened. Pour sauce over turnips and serve. Serves 4.

Crunchy Speckled Trout

¼ cup flour
4 egg whites, lightly beaten
½ cup crushed cornflakes
¼ cup fresh grated Parmesan cheese
4 (3½-ounce) speckled trout fillets
Mango, pineapple, or blackberry chutney

Preheat oven to 400°. Place flour in a small shallow bowl. Place egg in another small shallow bowl. Mix cornflakes and cheese in a 3rd shallow bowl. Roll fillets in flour, then egg, and then in cornflakes. Brown both sides in a non-stick skillet. Place on a baking sheet and bake 5 to 10 minutes or until flesh is firm. Spoon chutney onto each serving. Serves 4.

Speckled Trout Crêpes with Newburg Sauce

4 eggs
1 cup water
1 cup flour
⅓ cup butter plus more as needed for cooking
⅓ onion, minced
1 garlic clove, minced
½ teaspoon salt
¼ teaspoon white pepper
⅓ cup flour
1⅓ cups milk
⅔ cup inexpensive white wine
4 cups cooked speckled trout pieces
Instant Newburg Sauce

Make crêpes by whisking eggs and water then adding flour. Cover and refrigerate 2 hours. Brush butter on a hot skillet, pour in ¼ cup batter; tilt skillet around to make a thin crepe. When bottom begins to lightly brown, flip and brown other side. Remove and place a piece of wax paper on top. Repeat process using all batter. Should make 20 crêpes. Melt ⅓ cup butter and sauté onion and garlic until clear. Remove from heat and stir in salt, pepper and flour; cook over low heat until simmering. Whisk in milk and wine, return to a simmer for 1 minute stirring constantly. Remove from heat and gently mix in trout. Place 2 tablespoons of mixture on each crepe, roll up, and bake at 350° 10 minutes. Cover with remaining filling and Newburg Sauce.

To Roast the Wild Hog

There are three types of pigs in America: the familiar domestic breeds, the feral hog, and the European wild boar. Spanish settlers imported the original stock of domestic pigs to America in the mid 1500's. Many of these swine escaped or were raised under semi-wild conditions and after five hundred years of living and breeding in the wild their repressive traits, such as large razor-sharp tusks and long body hair have reappeared. Light colored hair has disappeared and has reverted to black or russet. Modern feral hogs appear in most states, the older strains have lost their domestic traits, and they have readily bread with the old Spanish stock. In 1912, George Moore imported a small herd of huge true European wild boars into his North Carolina animal preserve. These animals escaped, bred, and are now hunted in the Carolinas, Georgia, and as far North as Pennsylvania. Any shoat or wild hog weighting up to 80 pounds dressed weight will provide quality pork for roasting.

Cajun-Roasted Wild Hog

1 teaspoon mustard powder
1 teaspoon thyme
2 teaspoons paprika
3 teaspoons white pepper
1 teaspoon cayenne pepper
2 teaspoons salt
1 wild hog hindquarter
2 cups chopped onion
1 cup chopped green bell pepper
1 cup chopped celery
2 tablespoons chopped garlic

Combine seasonings and rub ¼ into the hindquarter. Place hindquarter in a racked roasting pan and brown all sides under the broiler. When brown, remove from heat and pour drippings into a large saucepan. Add remaining ingredients and simmer 5 minutes. Make numerous small cuts in the hindquarter, return to roasting pan, cover with sauce and bake at 350° until internal temperature reaches 150°. Turn twice and baste frequently with drippings. Serves 8 to 10.

Wild Hog Chili

3 slices thick-cut bacon, chopped
1 large onion, finely chopped
3 pounds wild hog meat, medium grind
1 quart beer or water
1 (4-ounce) can chopped green chilies
1 tablespoon crushed cumin seeds
⅔ cup prepared chili mix seasoning
1 quart tomato juice
1 tablespoon Tabasco sauce (optional)
½ cup yellow cornmeal or mesa

Sauté bacon and onion until onions are clear; add meat and brown. Combine 1½ cups beer, chilies, cumin, and chili mix in a large pot; simmer until thickened. Add meat, tomato juice, and Tabasco; simmer 2 to 3 hours. Scrape bottom frequently to prevent burning. Add more water if needed. Add cornmeal last 20 minutes. Serves 6.

Glazed Wild Hog Meatballs

1½ pounds wild hog, finely ground
¼ cup dry breadcrumbs
¼ cup chopped onion
1 teaspoon salt
½ teaspoon cinnamon
¼ teaspoon pepper
1½ cups grape or crab-apple jelly
½ cup ketchup

Combine all ingredients except jelly and ketchup. Roll into ¾-inch balls. Place jelly and ketchup in a skillet and simmer meatballs 25 minutes on low heat. Turn several times. Serve as warm appetizers from a heated dish.

Javelina Lemon Chops

4 thin-sliced wild hog chops
½ lemon, juiced
4 garlic cloves, crushed
Olive oil
1 tablespoon flour
½ cup chicken broth
Salt and pepper

Marinate chops in lemon juice and garlic; refrigerate 6 to 8 hours. Remove chops and fry in olive oil over medium heat until firm. Mix flour with chicken broth, add to chops, and cook until sauce thickens. Season to taste. Serves 2.

What Color is Your Bass?

Have you ever had one of those days when every bass you caught was within ounces of weighing the same and were caught in the same area? Like-sized bass tend to congregate and your knowledge of where to fish will be your key to whether or not you catch enough fish to fry for dinner. This is where the color of your fish is important. Depending on their surroundings, fish can and do change color. Look closely at the color of the first bass you catch. The color is a dead give-away as to the habitat that your bass has been living in. Dark colored bass are orientated to areas heavy in dark grass. A lighter-colored bass probably came from a sandy bottom. Bass who live under structures such as docks or houseboats tend to have a muted gray color. Once you determine the type of habitat your bass live in, look around for that type of habitat and concentrate casting in those areas.

Oriental Stuffed Bass

⅔ cup orange juice, divided
1 teaspoon teriyaki or soy sauce
4 teaspoons butter, divided
1 teaspoon minced ginger
1 small carrot, grated
1 green onion, finely chopped
1 cup stuffing mix
2 (8- to 10-ounce) bass fillets
2 orange peels
2 parsley sprigs

Preheat oven to 275°. Reserve 2 tablespoons orange juice. Simmer remaining juice, teriyaki sauce, 3 teaspoons butter, ginger, and carrot until it boils. Stir in onion and stuffing, remove from heat, and set aside 5 minutes. Spoon stuffing onto fillets, fold over and secure with a toothpick. Place in a baking dish, cover with remaining butter and orange juice. Bake 5 to 6 minutes, turn and cook another 4 to 5 minutes or until flesh is firm. Garnish with orange twists and parsley. Serves 2.

Mexican Bass Fillets

1 small tomato, chopped
½ cup chopped onion
½ cup chopped green pepper
¼ cup butter
¼ cup green chili salsa
2 tablespoons lemon juice
3 tablespoons sliced black olives
1 tablespoon chopped fresh parsley
1 garlic clove, finely chopped
Salt and Tabasco sauce
2 pounds bass fillets
¼ cup white wine or white grape juice

Preheat oven to 300°. Mix all ingredients, except fish and wine, in a 9x13-inch baking dish; bake 10 minutes. Add fillets and wine. Cover and cook 20 minutes or until flesh is firm. Delicious served with boiled rice. Serves 6.

Broiled Bass

1 pound bass fillets
3 tablespoons butter, melted
3 tablespoons lemon juice
2 tablespoons parsley flakes
Paprika

Spray broiler pan with non-stick spray; place bass in pan and cover with butter and lemon juice. Sprinkle with parsley and paprika. Broil until top is golden brown and flesh is firm, about 10 minutes. Serves 4.

Spiced Walnut Bass

2 pounds fillets
Salt and pepper
1½ cups ground walnuts
½ teaspoon thyme leaves
1 teaspoon marjoram leaves
1½ teaspoons chopped rosemary
1½ cups unseasoned breadcrumbs
1 cup flour
2 eggs, beaten
⅓ cup butter
⅓ cup cooking oil
Lemon wedges for garnish

Sprinkle fillets with salt and pepper. Mix walnuts, thyme, marjoram, rosemary, and breadcrumbs. Dredge fish in flour, dip in eggs, and roll in spice mixture. Heat butter and oil in a skillet and fry fish on each side until flesh is firm. Garnish with lemon wedges. Serves 6.

French Racks and Rib Steaks

French racks and rib steaks come from the same part of the deer — the section of the back over the ribs. The process begins by first sawing off the fore-part of the deer just in front of the first rib, then saw off the rib cage just behind the last rib and finally saw down the backbone to separate the two sides. The difference between rib steaks and French racks is that in rib steaks, the ribs are cut off and a saw cut is made across the backbone and loin into 1- to 1½-inch-thick steaks. French racks contain a whole loin and 6 to 8 inches of rib from which the connective tissue between each rib has been scraped off leaving the loin with a row of clean ribs. French racks are cooked whole and individual streaks are cut off at the table. Cook both to medium rare (138 degrees).

Venison French Rack with Blackberry Sauce

½ cup fresh or frozen blackberries
½ cup rice wine or white vinegar
2 tablespoons dark brown sugar
¼ teaspoon ground cinnamon
⅛ teaspoon ground nutmeg
⅛ teaspoon ground cloves
⅛ teaspoon red pepper or to taste
¼ teaspoon salt
Olive oil
1 (8-rib) venison French rack

Rub blackberries through a fine sieve or a food mill. In a small saucepan, combine all ingredients except oil and venison; cook until slightly thickened; cover and set aside. Rub venison with oil; insert a meat thermometer; cover bone tips with aluminum foil and bake in 300° oven until thermometer reaches 138°. Remove venison; wrap in aluminum foil and allow to rest 10 minutes. Place rack on a serving platter. At the table, slice off between ribs and spoon blackberry sauce over each serving. Serves 4.

Caribbean Venison Rib Steaks

3 tablespoons vegetable shortening
1 pound venison rib steaks
1½ tablespoons red wine vinegar
1 tablespoon ground cinnamon
1 tablespoon ground ginger
1 tablespoon ground nutmeg
1 teaspoon salt
¼ teaspoon black pepper
1½ cups water
3 cups apple juice
1 can condensed tomato soup
1 cup chopped onion
1 teaspoon chopped garlic

Melt shortening in a large heavy pot and brown venison. Whisk together vinegar, cinnamon, ginger, nutmeg, salt and pepper. Add water and apple juice and pour over venison. Spoon tomato soup, onion and garlic on top of venison. Cover and simmer 4 hours or until tender. If needed, thicken gravy with more flour. Serves 4.

J. with the blood of her first deer — a longtime custom of deer hunters.

Chevreuil Steaks à la Janelle

2 to 3 tablespoons canola oil
8 small venison rib steaks
Salt and pepper
½ teaspoon paprika
1 green onion, chopped
2 tablespoons chopped white onion
Pinch ground oregano
1 garlic clove, mashed
2 tablespoons chopped fresh parsley, divided
½ cup cream
3 tablespoons Brandy or Cognac
3 tablespoons Madeira or Port
2 egg yolks, beaten

Heat oil in a large skillet over medium heat. Sprinkle venison with salt, pepper and paprika. Sauté steaks in oil until brown on both sides. Add onions, oregano, garlic and 1 tablespoon parsley. Cover and simmer 10 minutes or until venison is tender. If mixture looks dry, add a little water. Remove venison to a serving platter and cover with foil. Combine cream, Brandy, Madeira and egg yolks; whisk into skillet juices. Cook over very low heat, stirring constantly, until slightly thickened. Pour sauce over venison and sprinkle with remaining parsley. Serves 4 to 6.

Fresh Caught or Farm Raised

Fifty-million pounds of catfish are grown on catfish farms each year. What is the difference between farm-raised catfish and catfish I catch on my trotlines? Generally speaking not much—specifically, a great deal. From my experience, natural catfish don't taste much different from the farm-raised variety. The difference as I see is in the price, the availability, convenience, and consistency in size. I don't know how much my natural catfish cost me, but when you consider the gas, time spent going, coming, and running the lines, and not to mention the skinning—farm-raised catfish have to be a great deal less expensive. What I like about farm-raised catfish is that I can purchase as much or as little as I need and at any time I wish. When I am frying up a mess of catfish and hushpuppies for a yard full of people, the convenience and consistent size does make the job much easier. With all that being said, the joy of bringing home a chest full of your own catch and walking into the kitchen with a pan full of fresh-out-of-the-water fillets is spiritually inexpensive at twice the price.

Grilled Catfish Oriental

2 teaspoons teriyaki or light soy sauce
¼ teaspoon red pepper flakes (optional)
3 tablespoons dry white wine (optional)
1 pound catfish fillets
Chopped cilantro for garnish

Combine teriyaki sauce, red pepper and wine. Place in a plastic bag along with catfish and marinate 45 minutes in refrigerator. Grill on both sides or broil for 5 to 8 minutes or until flesh is firm. Baste often. Garnish with cilantro. Serves 4.

Broiled Catfish with Mustard and Pecan Crust

1¼ pounds catfish fillets
Salt and pepper
3 tablespoons Dijon mustard
4 lemon wedges
⅓ cup toasted and chopped pecans
2 tablespoons chopped green onion tops

Spray baking dish with non-stick spray and lay in fillets. Sprinkle with salt and pepper. Cover with mustard and broil 5 minutes or until flesh is firm. Arrange on serving plates with a lemon wedge and sprinkle with pecans and green onions. Serves 4.

Catfish and Bacon Salad

½ each red and yellow bell pepper
2 catfish fillets, cubed 1-inch
Water
¼ cup olive oil
¼ cup balsamic or rice wine vinegar
1 small red onion, sliced
1½ teaspoons dried dill weed
1 head Boston or other lettuce, torn
2 cups arugula or romaine lettuce, torn
4 pieces bacon, cooked and crumbled
⅓ cup blue, Stilton or Roquefort cheese
Salt and pepper

Preheat oven to 350°. Place bell pepper in oven for 10 minutes or until soft. Cut into strips and reserve. In a large skillet, cover catfish with water, bring to a boil and simmer until flesh begins to firm. Remove catfish, drain and place in a large salad bowl. Mix in olive oil, vinegar, onion, dill and pepper strips. Cover and refrigerate 1 hour. Mix in lettuce, bacon and cheese. Season with salt and pepper. Serves 4.

Broiled Catfish with Orange Sauce

¼ cup fresh orange juice
2 tablespoons cooking oil
2 tablespoons teriyaki or soy sauce
1 tablespoon fresh lemon juice
1 garlic clove, minced
⅛ teaspoon black pepper
4 pounds catfish fillets

Combine all ingredients except catfish. Place in a plastic bag along with catfish and marinate 15 minutes in refrigerator. Broil or grill 5 minutes on each side until flesh begins to firm. Baste often with marinade. Serves 4.

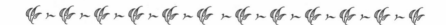

Who Says You Can't Broil Venison

Venison can be broiled and is absolutely delicious. But I need to qualify that statement by saying that not all cuts of venison are candidates for broiling anymore than all cuts of beef are able to be broiled. Since venison has virtually no marbling, you have to choose your cut and cooking methods carefully. The best primal cut for broiling is the loin (backstrap) when it is cut across-the-grain into 1¼-inch thick pieces. When turned on their sides the pieces settle down to 1-inch thick pieces which are the perfect thickness for broiling. Next, soak the pieces of venison in olive or other oil for a few minutes. Cook to no more than medium and preferably a little less than medium or 138° internal temperature on a meat thermometer. If cooked to well done the meat will firm up and will be tough not be tender or juicy. Lastly, allow the finished pieces to rest for a few minutes before serving so that the juices settle down. This resting period allows the center to continue cooking and when cut, the juices will remain inside.

Broiled Venison Steak Leopold

(A variation of a circa 1790 beef steak recipe by King Leopold I of Belgium)

1 aged venison top round steak, 1½-inches thick
Salt
Fresh ground black pepper
1½ tablespoons real butter, softened
½ ounce hot brandy

Salt one side of the steak and then grind on a generous portion of black pepper. Press the salt and pepper into the steak. Turn steak over and repeat on other side. Broil steak on both sides to rare or not more than medium rare. Spread the butter over the top of the steak and place in the oven until the butter just begins to melt. Remove steak, pour over with hot brandy and serve immediately. Serves 2 to 4.

Venison Steak Florentine

4 tablespoons olive oil
2 tablespoons minced parsley
2 garlic cloves, minced
½ teaspoon salt
½ teaspoon pepper
1 tablespoon lemon juice
1 (1½- to 2-inch) venison steak cut from top of hindquarter
1 large lump of warm butter
1 lemon, cut into wedges
1 tomato, cut into wedges

Combine olive oil, parsley, garlic, salt, pepper and 1 tablespoon lemon juice in a large zip-lock bag. Marinate steak in refrigerator for 3 hours. Remove steak and broil on both sides to no more than medium (138°). Serve on a large platter with several lumps of warm butter on top. Garnish with parsley sprigs, lemon and tomato wedges. Serves 2 to 4.

Broiled Whole Venison Loin

1 venison loin with silver skin removed
2 teaspoons garlic salt
1½ teaspoons black pepper
1 stick butter

Score venison with a sharp knife diagonally several times across the loin. Rub garlic salt and pepper into the meat. Place meat on a broiling pan and sear both sides. Place pads of butter on top and continue to broil until a meat thermometer just reaches 138°. Wrap in aluminum foil and allow to rest several minutes. Slice thin and serve. Serves 8.

Fettuccine Béarnaise Venison

4 pieces venison loin, 1¼-inch thick
¼ cup Worcestershire sauce
Cooked fettuccine for 4
Instant Béarnaise Sauce
Paprika

Place loin slices and Worcestershire sauce in a zip-lock bag and refrigerate one hour. Broil or grill on both sides to no more than medium. Serve on a bed of fettuccine and cover with Béarnaise Sauce. Sprinkle with paprika. Serves 4.

Come Gather at Our Table

For over a half century, I have had the pleasure of being invited to gather at many deer camp tables for the traditional Thanksgiving dinner. I cannot remember the year when the hand of hospitality has not been extended. Whether it was at Electric Mills, Leakesville, Deeth, Baxley, or any other place that I happened upon, I have always been welcomed and my plate has always run over. The tradition of welcoming family, friends, guests, and walk-in strangers to sit at the deer camp table and give thanks together is one of the glues that bind us and our traditions together. It is the sitting at the table, the breaking of the bread, and the fellowship that make those moments last a lifetime. I cannot recall what gifts I received from Santa Claus when I was a child, but I can remember each and every Thanksgiving at deer camp — the people and the food have bound those memories deep inside of me.

Dessert table for Thanksgiving in Leakesville.

French Onion Venison Roast

Go to work, and dinner will be ready when you get home.

1 (3-pound) boneless venison roast
6 small potatoes
6 medium onions
2 cloves garlic, chopped
2 bay leaves
⅛ teaspoon Tabasco sauce
¼ teaspoon pepper
2 cans French onion soup
Salt and pepper
Prepared rice for 4 to 6

Place venison roast in a 6-quart crockpot; add remaining ingredients except rice. Set to low and cook 8 hours. Serve over cooked rice. Serves 4 to 6.

Johnny Cake

The bread that both won and lost The War.

1 cup yellow cornmeal
1 cup all-purpose flour
½ teaspoon salt
½ teaspoon baking soda
2 cups sour whole milk
2 eggs
3 tablespoons sorghum or black-strap molasses

Preheat oven to 400°. Mix and sift together cornmeal, flour, and salt. Add baking soda to sour milk and stir until it foams; add dry mixture. Beat together eggs and molasses and mix into batter. Pour into a 9x12-inch oiled baking pan. Bake 20 minutes or until golden brown. Serves 8 to 10.

Baked Beans

An authentic 1794 Colonial American recipe.

4 cups dried pea beans
1 large onion, studded with 8 cloves
½ pound salt pork
1 cup dark brown sugar, divided
3 teaspoons dry mustard
2 teaspoons salt
1 teaspoon pepper
½ cup dark molasses

Preheat oven to 250°. Soak beans overnight. Place drained beans in a large saucepan, cover with water, and cook until skins burst when blown on. Drain beans, place in a ceramic bean pot, press onion into center of beans until covered. Chunk salt pork and push pieces into beans. Pour ¾ cup brown sugar, mustard, salt, pepper, and molasses over beans. Stir gently adding enough boiling water to cover beans. Cover and bake 4 to 5 hours. Uncover last half hour. Sprinkle with remaining brown sugar. Add water as needed while baking. Serves 10 to 12.

Southern Pecan Pie

John C. Stennis, Mississippi United States Senator 1946 to 1988

3 eggs, beaten
1 cup sugar
1 cup corn syrup
½ teaspoon salt
1 teaspoon vanilla
1 cup pecan halves
1 (9-inch) pie shell, unbaked

Preheat oven to 300°. Beat eggs and sugar until thick. Add corn syrup, salt, vanilla, and pecan halves. Pour into pie shell and bake 50 to 60 minutes or until filling is set. Serves 6 to 8.

Cooking-up the Whole Big Bass

Last week my good friend and neighbor, Mr. Icey, brought me four of the nicest largemouth bass that you have ever seen and I did something with them that I have always wanted to do. Being rather partial to coastal Mediterranean and Portuguese cuisine, I scaled and gutted the bass, removed the gills, vacuum packed, and froze my windfall with the heads still on. I have been served world class rainbow trout in butter-lemon sauce with the heads on and I have eaten delicious baked whole sea bass in Samoa that still had the head attached. But, I have never tried to bake, grill, or roast whole largemouth bass. Now I don't recommend this for everyone. But somehow, I have always enjoyed watching a large platter, containing a whole fish, surrounded by all the accompanying garnishments being ceremoniously brought to the table along with a loaf of crusty bread and a bottle of the local wine. The atmosphere is relaxed, the company is jovial and the food is always good. Just the thought of it makes me want to take my shirt and shoes off, roll up my pant legs and retire as a carefree fisherman on some remote Greek island.

Mr. Icey
bringing over
the whole big bass.

Onion-Stuffed Baked Bass

1 large whole bass
2 onions, finely chopped
3 cups seasoned breadcrumbs
2 eggs, lightly beaten
1 tomato, skinned and finely chopped
2 teaspoons chopped parsley
Salt and pepper
2 cups water

Preheat oven to 360°. From inside body cavity, cut rib bones away from each side of backbone and carefully remove rib bones. Slice down on one side of the backbone to make a cavity. Combine remaining ingredients, except water, and stuff bass. Place bass in a greased baking dish, cover with water and bake 30 minutes. Serves 2 to 4.

Spicy Italian Stuffed Bass

1 large whole bass
Salt, pepper and garlic powder
Juice of 2 to 4 lemons
½ stick butter
1 large onion, chopped
1 green bell pepper, chopped
2 cans tomato sauce
1 can whole tomatoes
2 cups water
Dash Tabasco sauce (optional)
1 cup white wine or water
¼ cup chopped parsley
¼ cup chopped green onions tops
Lemon slices

Preheat oven to 320°. Season fish with salt, pepper and garlic powder. Marinate 2 hours in lemon juice. Melt butter and gently sauté onions and pepper until just tender. Add tomato sauce and tomatoes, simmer 45 minutes. Add water and Tabasco sauce; simmer 25 minutes. Mix in wine. Place fish in a large casserole dish and cover with tomato mixture. Bake 40 minutes or until flesh is firm. Sprinkle with parsley and onion. Garnish with lemon slices. Serves 4 to 6.

Baked Bass Fillets with Avocado Sauce

1 avocado, chopped
¼ cup milk
1 tablespoon lime juice
1 garlic clove, minced
Dash Tabasco sauce (optional)
2 tablespoons lemon juice
1 teaspoon lemon zest
1 tablespoon teriyaki or soy sauce
1 teaspoon Dijon mustard
1½ pounds large bass fillets
⅓ cup breadcrumbs

Mix first 5 ingredients, process until smooth and set aside. Mix lemon juice and zest, soy sauce, and mustard. Dip fish in the lemon mixture and then dredge in the breadcrumbs. Place fillets on baking sheet prepared with non-stick spray. Bake 7 minutes, turn over and bake another 7 minutes or until flesh is just firm. Serve covered with avocado sauce. Serves 2 to 4 .

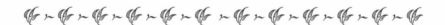

Tilapia: A Biblical Fish but Raised in the South

If you have never eaten tilapia, you should try it. Tilapia was one of the first fish cultivated and is called "St. Peter's Fish" because of the biblical reference to it as the fish used to feed the multitudes. Egyptian paintings suggest Tilapia were farmed from the Nile more than 3,000 years ago. Tilapia aquaculture has spread around the world because they are easy to raise in man-made ponds, are disease-resistant, are quick growing, and eat a wide range of vegetation, from plankton to high-protein fish feeds. Today, some of the catfish farmers in the South are raising larger and larger quantities of tilapia. Many grocery and discount stores offer tilapia in their frozen foods section. Because of its minimal number of bones, it is a popular fillet fish which can be baked, pan-fried, grilled or used in stews and soups. Tilapia and can be substituted in most fish recipes.

Broiled Tilapia with Lemon-Parmesan Sauce

2½ pounds tilapia fillets
3 teaspoons butter, softened
2 teaspoons plus 2 tablespoons lemon juice
1 cup mayonnaise
½ cup grated Parmesan cheese
Fresh basil and sliced lemons for garnish

Top fillets with butter and 2 teaspoons lemon juice; broil 5 to 8 minutes until flesh is firm. Mix together mayonnaise, 2 tablespoons lemon juice and Parmesan cheese. Place 1 tablespoon on each fillet; broil 2 minutes or until toppings puff and begin to brown. Garnish with basil and sliced lemon. Serves 6.

Grilled Tilapia with Spicy Oyster Sauce

½ teaspoon salt
1 tablespoon minced garlic
½ teaspoon black pepper
1 tablespoon anchovy paste
¼ cup olive or other oil
1 whole (2- to 3-pound) tilapia
1 tablespoon oyster sauce
1½ tablespoons teriyaki or soy sauce
1 teaspoon sugar
1 tablespoon ketchup
½ teaspoon Tabasco sauce
¼ teaspoon curry powder

Combine first 5 ingredients and marinate fish 10 minutes. Combine remaining ingredients to make a sauce and set aside. Grill fillets on both sides until flesh is firm. Serve with sauce. Serves 4.

Baked Tilapia in Raspberry Sauce

¼ cup honey
¼ cup raspberry vinegar
¼ cup olive oil
1 teaspoon mustard
½ teaspoon dried dill
4 ounces tilapia fillets

Preheat oven to 350°. Grease a baking dish with shortening. Whisk together all ingredients except fillets. Place fillets in baking dish and cover with sauce. Bake 20 minutes or until flesh is firm. Serves 2.

Sautéed Tilapia with Lime-Butter Sauce

Salt and pepper
5 tablespoons flour
10 ounces tilapia fillets
1 tablespoon lime juice
½ tablespoon butter
½ cup white wine
1 garlic clove, minced
1 tablespoon olive oil
3 green onions, chopped

Mix salt and pepper into flour and dredge fillets. Combine lime juice, butter, wine and garlic and set aside. Heat oil in a sauté pan and cook fillets until just brown; turn and cook until flesh is just firm; remove to serving platter. Add lime mixture to pan, scrape up bits and reduce by half. Stir in onions and sauté 30 seconds. Pour sauce over fillets and serve. Serves 4.

Sausage Rats

The word "smokehouse" conjures up images of a forbidden, old wooden out-building sitting out back next to the corncrib. Forbidden because I was threatened with life and limb if you were ever caught opening the door. The sweet-smoky aroma was so overpowering that you just could not help yourself. What I remember most about Mr. Brown's smokehouse is the coiled links of brownish-red smoked sausages looped over the steel rods. The smell was debilitating. I stretched up and carefully pinched off a small piece of sausage and chewed it until it was gone. I looked outside to make sure that no one was around and I pinched off a larger piece and then another big piece. Several days later Mom sent me over to Mrs. Brown's house to see if she had any fresh butter for sale. While I sat in the kitchen waiting for her to scoop up the butter, Mr. Brown came in. He sat down on the bench beside me and looking up at the ceiling said, "Last month, I put some rat poison on one of the sausage links in the smokehouse just in case a sausage rat was able to find his way in. When he nibbles on that sausage he is going to be one dead sausage rat. It takes about a week or so for the poison to work. Harold Jr., tell your mother if she sees a dead sausage rat laying around her yard, she'll know what happened to him."

The original sausage rat.

Crêpes with Venison Sausage and Cream Cheese Sauce

½ pound ground venison sausage, crumbled
½ cup chopped green onions plus 1 large green onion, finely chopped
1½ cups shredded sharp Cheddar cheese, divided
2 tablespoons butter
4 large eggs, beaten
8 ounces cottage cheese, pureéd in food processor until smooth
8 to 10 crêpes
⅛ teaspoon each salt and ground pepper
1 cup heavy cream
1 tablespoon dry white wine
¼ teaspoon Dijon mustard
Pinch red pepper

Preheat oven to 350°. In a large skillet; cook venison sausage over medium heat for about 15 minutes until brown. Remove sausage to a medium bowl. Reserve 2 tablespoons of the drippings. Add ½ cup chopped green onions to skillet and cook over medium-high heat until just tender; add to venison sausage. Stir in 1 cup Cheddar cheese. In a separate skillet; melt butter over very low heat. Add eggs and cook slowly until just beginning to set. Remove from stove and allow to slightly cool. Stir pureéd cottage cheese into eggs. Fold egg mixture into venison sausage mixture. Place ⅓ cup filling down the enter of each crepe and roll up. Place crêpes in a baking pan seam down and cover with foil. Bake 2 minutes or until heated through. While crêpes are cooking, make the Cream Cheese Sauce. In a medium saucepan; mix together cream, wine, and remaining green onions. Reduce to ¾ cup or until the sauce lightly coats the back of a spoon. Stir in mustard and red pepper. Stir in ½ cup Cheddar cheese until melted. Spoon over baked crêpes and serve. Serves 4 to 5.

Slow-Cooked Spicy Venison and Rice Stew

1 teaspoon cooking oil
2 pounds spicy venison link sausage, casing removed
2 cloves garlic, minced
2 teaspoons ground cumin
4 onions, chopped
4 green bell peppers, chopped
3 jalapeño peppers, seeded and minced
4 cups beef broth
2 (6¼-ounce) packages long-grain and wild rice mix

Heat cooking oil in large skillet. Add venison sausage and break up while cooking. Cook about 5 minutes or until browned. Add garlic and cumin; cook 30 seconds. Add onion, bell pepper, and jalapeño pepper. Sauté about 10 minutes until onions are just clear. Pour mixture into crockpot. Stir in beef broth and rice; cook on low 4 hours. Serves 10 to 12.

Sour Cream and Venison Sausage Omelets

8 ounces link venison sausage, casings removed and cut into bite-size pieces
2 tablespoons chopped green onions
½ cup sour cream
4 eggs, beaten
2 tablespoons water
½ teaspoon celery salt
1 tablespoon canola oil

Cook sausage and onions in skillet until sausage is browned. Remove and drain on paper towels. Leave sausage drippings in skillet. Place sausage in a bowl and mix in sour cream. Whisk eggs with water and celery salt until well blended. Heat sausage drippings over medium-high heat. Pour ½ of egg mixture into skillet. Using spatula, lift eggs as they cook, letting uncooked part run underneath until omelet is cooked but still creamy. Spoon ½ of sausage mixture over half of omelet. Slide out onto plate, folding omelet over filling. Keep warm. Heat oil in same skillet and repeat the process for second omelet. Serve immediately. Serves 2.

Ol' Roy was a Pointing Dog

From what I remember, Ol' Roy was a sheepdog and spent most of his time riding on the front seat of "Dog" Owens pick-up truck, with his head out the window and his tongue waving in the wind. Whenever I saw that black pick-up truck come flying down our dirt road, I could always count on seeing Ol' Roy looking out the window and pointing his long tongue out at me as he sped by. I would wave and holler until the cloud of rolling dust engulfed me and blurred out the truck. I would stand there eating dirt and hoping he would stop and come back so I could play with Ol' Roy. "Dog" was never one to stop and talk—unless he had something important to say. One morning I concocted a plan where by I would telephone "Dog" and tell him my grandfather needed to talk to him about the hogs they were going to slaughter in a few weeks. Fortunately for me, I told my grandfather what I had in mind and why. He stopped cooking breakfast, put his hand on my head and said, "Harold, Jr., how did you know I was needing to talk to him about the hogs? You, just go ahead and give him a call for me, would you?" As I look back now, I am sure he did not need to talk about the hogs, but he knew I needed to play with Ol' Roy. To this day, I can't pass by a sheepdog without stopping for a little hug.

Harold hugging another
Ol' Roy in Scotland.

Creamy Grits

3 cups half-and-half
¾ cup Quaker Quick Grits
¼ teaspoon salt

Bring half-and-half to a slight boil; slowly stir in grits and salt. Reduce heat to medium-low and cover. Cook, stirring occasionally, 5 to 7 minutes or until thickened. Serve with cheese, butter, red-eye gravy or as a hot cereal with milk and sugar. Serves 4.

Buttermilk Yeast Biscuits

2 packages dry yeast
¼ cup warm water
2 cups buttermilk
5 cups all-purpose flour plus more for rolling dough
¼ cup sugar
1 tablespoon baking powder
1 teaspoon salt
1 cup lard or vegetable shortening

Combine yeast with warm water and let stand 5 minutes. Add buttermilk and set aside. Combine 5 cups flour, sugar, baking powder, and salt. Cut shortening into dry ingredients until mixture is the size of coarse meal. Add buttermilk mixture, stirring with a fork. Turn dough out onto a floured surface and gently knead 3 or 4 times. Roll dough to ½-inch thickness and cut straight down with a 2½-inch cutter. Place biscuits on a lightly greased baking sheet, cover and let rise in a warm place for 1 hour. Bake in a 450° preheated oven 10 to 12 minutes or until golden brown.

Red-Eye Gravy

3 tablespoons left-over salted ham or bacon fat
1½ cups strong black coffee
Salt and pepper

Heat fat and bottom scrapings in a heavy skillet. Stir in coffee. Salt and pepper to taste. Serve over grits, mashed potatoes or venison. Serves 4.

Frying-up the Small Bass

I would much prefer to catch a dozen small bass, than one big lunker, as I have never been much for having a stuffed fish hanging on my wall. But I sure do like to have a bunch of those small ones in my stomach. Miss Anne would prefer not to eat small bass because the small bones give her a problem. I appreciate her dislike for bones, but I also appreciate my preference for small bass. Over the years we have stopped fussing over it and we have struck a happy medium. I cook fillets all year long for Miss Anne. And in return, Miss Anne allows me to fry-up whole small bass twice a year. I suppose the reason I like small bass cooked this way is that they stay moist and do not dry out as the thinner fillets sometimes have a tendency to do. Maybe it is just my imagination, but the flesh is tastier and moister when a piece of fried fish is thicker. This probably goes back to my up-bringing when my dad would always fry-up his small bass in one piece and in her youth, Miss Anne was always served fillets.

Fried Small Bass

½ cup flour
2 (¾-pound) small bass
¼ teaspoon salt
⅛ teaspoon pepper
½ cup butter, divided
1 cup sliced mushrooms
¼ cup chopped green onions
2 tablespoons white wine
1 tablespoon lemon juice

Place flour on a large plate. Season bass with salt and pepper. Roll fish in flour inside and out. Melt 2 tablespoons butter in a skillet and fry bass until flesh is just firm. Remove, cover and set aside. Melt remaining butter; sauté mushrooms and onion until just tender, about 3 minutes. Stir in wine and lemon juice and pour over fish. Serves 2.

Mashed Potatoes and Turnips

2 potatoes, peeled and sliced
2 turnips, peeled and sliced
2 cups chopped turnip greens
1 tablespoon minced garlic
2 tablespoons olive oil
Salt, pepper and Tabasco sauce

Boil potatoes and turnips in lightly salted water. Drain and mash. Place in a saucepan and keep warm. Sauté greens and garlic in olive oil about 10 minutes or until wilted. Purée in a food processor and stir into potato mixture. Season with salt, pepper and Tabasco sauce to taste. Serves 4.

Stalking the Wild Fall Turkey

For many parts of the country, November is the beginning of the fall turkey season. This season adds an additional dimension to the sport. Fall turkey regulations may allow for the harvest of either sex and may also allow no beard limits on gobblers. I enjoy the fall season because, for miles around I may be the only turkey hunter in the woods and that means that my harvesting odds are better. I enjoy the opportunity to sit on the cool ground and enjoy the quiet fall air. You don't hunt fall turkeys like you do the spring turkey. Fall turkeys have split into groups of hens, jakes, and gobblers. Each morning the individual groups re-establish their pecking order. When they first fly down from their roost there is much squabbling amongst the birds until everyone is in their proper place. This is where your scouting is critical because you need to know what type of group you are working. You then enter into the pecking-order-calling contest. At some point the dominant bird will realize that you have not come under their control. The fun begins when the flock responds to your call and runs toward you.

Turkey Chow Mein Casserole

3 cups chopped cooked turkey
¼ cup chopped onion
¼ cup chopped bell pepper
½ cup chopped celery
1 (2-ounce) jar sliced pimento, drained
1 (4-ounce) can mushroom pieces
½ teaspoon poultry seasoning
1 cup whole milk
2 cans cream of mushroom soup
1 (3-ounce) can chow mein noodles

Preheat oven to 325°. Grease a 2-quart casserole dish with butter. Combine turkey, onion, pepper, celery, pimento, mushrooms, and seasoning. Mix together milk and mushroom soup; pour over casserole. Cover with noodles and bake 30 minutes. Serves 4 to 6.

Chilled Turkey Salad

1½ cups left-over turkey pieces
¼ cup chopped fresh parsley
1 tablespoon chopped fresh rosemary
1 large apple or pear, cored and chopped
⅛ teaspoon salt
⅛ teaspoon white pepper
¼ cup mayonnaise
2 large lettuce leaves
1 cup bean or other sprouts
Fresh parsley and basil for garnish

Combine all ingredients except lettuce and sprouts. Cover and chill several hours. Place turkey mixture on lettuce and sprinkle with sprouts. Garnish with a parsley sprig and fresh basil. Serves 2.

Wild Turkey Chili

2 wild turkey breasts
1½ cups chopped onions
3 tablespoons oil
1 cup water
2 cans chicken broth
3 cans white beans
1 can whole corn
1 (4-ounce) can chilies, chopped (optional)
1 tablespoon chopped fresh parsley
⅛ teaspoon each garlic powder and ground cloves
¼ teaspoon each onion powder, celery salt, paprika, and oregano flakes
1 tablespoon ground cumin
Salt and pepper
Flour tortillas
1 cup shredded Cheddar cheese

Sauté turkey breasts and onions in oil until onions are clear. Add remaining ingredients; except cheese and tortillas. Simmer 1 to 2 hours over low heat. Serve on tortillas and top with cheese. Serves 4.

Wild Turkey Breakfast

1 wild turkey breast
½ cup flour
Salt and pepper
½ cup buttermilk
¼ cup each oil and real butter

Cut turkey breast into 1-inch-wide slices. Mix flour, salt, and pepper in a paper bag. Dip turkey strips in buttermilk; add to bag and shake to cover. Heat oil and butter and fry until brown. Serve with brown gravy, biscuits, sorghum molasses, sliced tomato, and coffee. Serves 4.

Thanksgiving at Deer Camp

Thanksgiving at deer camp is as much a right of passage as a celebration. Friends, families, and guests come together to celebrate the bounty of the summer and the coming of winter, but it is a right of passage because it is a point from which time is measured. My first Thanksgiving at deer camp was at the now defunct village of Electric Mills. The name was rather a misnomer because we had no electricity in camp; kerosene lanterns provided light and cooking was done on a old wood stove. What I remember most was the food. Or, should I say the preparation of the food. I spent the mornings getting in the way of the cooks as they prepared dish after dish on the huge black stove. I was amazed at how they would raise the heat in the oven with small pieces of wood for one dish and lower the temperature for another dish with larger pieces of wood. To keep me occupied and out of the way, they sat me on a lard bucket and fed me halves of breakfast-biscuits filled with homemade butter and sorghum molasses. Closer to lunch I was given biscuits with a small piece of chicken fried venison and brown gravy. When lunch was finally served, it no longer held my interest—until the cold bowls of banana pudding, hidden away in the ice-cooled refrigerator, were brought forth.

Chicken-Fried Venison Steak

1 to 1½ pounds boneless venison round steak, ½-inch thick
⅓ cup plus 1¼ cups milk, divided
1 egg
⅓ cup plus 2 tablespoons flour, divided
Salt and pepper
2 tablespoons each butter and vegetable oil
Cooked rice for 4

Pound steak to ¼-inch with meat mallet. Whisk ⅓ cup milk and egg in a bowl. In a separate bowl, mix ⅓ cup flour, ½ teaspoon salt, and ⅛ teaspoon pepper. Dip steaks in milk mixture, dredge in seasoned flour, and set aside. In skillet, melt butter and oil on medium-low heat. Brown steaks on both sides and set aside to drain. Whisk 2 tablespoons flour and ¼ teaspoon salt into 1¼ cups milk; season with pepper and mix into pan drippings. Stirring constantly, cook over medium heat until thickened. If too thick, add more milk. Serve gravy with steaks and cooked rice. Serves 4.

Baked Banana Pudding

1⅓ cups sugar, divided
½ cup flour
3 cups milk
4 eggs, separated
1 tablespoon plus 1 teaspoon vanilla extract, divided
3 tablespoons butter
1½ cups whipping cream
1 box vanilla wafers
7 bananas, sliced
¼ teaspoon cream of tartar

Whisk 1 cup sugar, flour and milk in heavy saucepan until smooth. Set over medium heat and cook, stirring constantly, just until mixture comes to boil. Remove from heat and whisk a little of the hot pudding into beaten yolks. Pour yolk mixture into pudding and whisk well. Cook 1 to 2 minutes, stirring until thick. Strain mixture and stir in 1 tablespoon vanilla and butter until it melts. Lay plastic wrap directly onto surface of pudding and refrigerate until chilled. Whip cream until stiff peaks form; fold into chilled pudding. Line an oven-proof dish with wafers. Top with ⅓ of the pudding, then half the bananas. Place another layer of wafers. Top with another third of pudding and remaining bananas. Top with layer of pudding. Preheat oven to 350°. Beat egg whites, cream of tartar and 1 teaspoon vanilla until stiff. Slowly add ⅓ cup sugar and beat until glossy. Spread meringue over top of pudding and bake until meringue is lightly golden, about 15 minutes. Serve cold. Serves 6 to 8.

The Accidental Trophy

I was and am a confirmed meat hunter. It was about this time last year when J. and I were hunting some hardwood bottoms that I first saw my "Accidental Trophy." As I watched, all I could see was that he was either an above average four pointer or possibly a small six. I finally decided that this was the one that I needed to make into T-bone steaks for dinner and a rolled and smoked hindquarter roast for Christmas. What a surprise when I walked out and counted ten points and more deer than I had bargained for. This was one deer that I had rather seen walk. I have taken my share of trophies and one of the joys of my life is to hunt with my niece in hopes of her harvesting her first trophy. When J. picked me up on her ATV, she corrected me, "Uncle Harold, its 11 points." It took J. and me over an hour to load that 230+ pound deer on her ATV and for the next three days, that deer owned me—until I was able to get every piece of it into the freezer. My "Accidental Trophy?" Oh, it's hanging on the wall.

Harold, J., Mr. Will, and the "accidental trophy."

Potato Salad with Smoked Venison Sausage

1½ pounds smoked venison link sausage
3 tablespoons white vinegar
⅓ cup olive oil
½ teaspoon salt
¼ teaspoon black pepper
2 pounds small red potatoes, cooked, pared, sliced
Lettuce leaves
⅓ cup sliced green onions with tops
2 tablespoons capers

Grill sausage until done and slice on the diagonal into ¼-inch thick pieces. Whisk together vinegar, oil, salt and pepper. Gently spoon potatoes into oil mixture and add sausage. Place lettuce leaves on individual serving plates and spoon on sausage and potatoes. Top with green onions and capers. Serves 4.

Corn and Venison Sausage Chowder

1 Polish-style or other venison sausage, thin slices
6 slices bacon, chopped
1 cup chopped onions
2 cups canned beef or chicken broth
1 cup cold water
¼ cup flour
4 cups whole kernel corn
2 cups cubed potatoes
⅛ teaspoon white pepper
Tabasco sauce
2 cups whole milk
4 tablespoons real butter, divided

In a soup pot, brown sausage and bacon until bacon is crisp. Remove and drain on paper towels. Discard all but 2 tablespoons fat. Sauté onions until just clear. Mix broth and water. Gradually sift and stir flour into broth; add to pot along with sausage, bacon, corn, potatoes, white pepper, and Tabasco sauce to taste. Heat to boiling. Reduce heat, cover, and simmer 15 to 20 minutes stirring occasionally. Add milk and cook until soup is heated and potatoes are tender. Serve in individual bowls topped with a dollop of butter. Serves 6 to 8.

Shrimp and Venison Sausage
with Mushroom Cream Sauce

2 tablespoons olive oil
12 ounces smoked venison sausage, sliced
20 large raw shrimp, peeled
16 large mushrooms, quartered
1 cup whipping cream
4 teaspoons Worcestershire sauce
Salt and pepper
Cooked rice for 4
Chopped fresh parsley

Heat olive oil in a skillet. Add venison sausage and cook until almost done. Add shrimp; sauté until shrimp just turn pink but are still soft. Remove shrimp and venison sausage; set aside. Add mushrooms to skillet and sauté until just tender. Stir in whipping cream and Worcestershire sauce. Simmer until sauce begins to thicken. Return shrimp and sausage to skillet and simmer until shrimp are just cooked, about 1 minute. Season with salt and pepper. Place cooked rice on serving platter, spoon on sausage and shrimp. Cover with mushroom sauce. Sprinkle with parsley and serve. Serves 4.

J. —Harold's best hunting bud.

Best Smallmouth Bass Fishing in the South

I never much thought about smallmouth bass until I moved to Arkansas in 1970. It was John Houston who introduced me to *Micropterus dolomieu* or as he called them: Brownies. We were to spend the day canoeing and searching for the white water rapids in the remote upper reaches of the Cossatot River before the Corps of Engineers dammed the river and the pristine landscape would be forever changed. John asked if I had brought my ultra-light rod with me. Silly me. I thought we were going to have a fine old day blasting through rapids and dodging boulders. When we came to the slow moving pools between the rapids, John fished and I paddled. At noon we pulled over to have lunch on one of the pristine sandbars under the bluffs. John asked me to build a little fire while he cleaned the fish. He sprinkled them with salt and pepper and squeezed on lemon juice. Then he wrapped them in aluminum foil and eased them into the coals. Fifteen minutes later I was in hog heaven. Smallmouth bass are found in lakes, but they are far more widespread and numerous in the less turbid waters of our smaller streams. During periods of high flows they disperse and use the rocky and log-fall habitat. As water levels recede they are forced into the deeper pools of water. When choosing smallmouth baits, think small. Use number 0 or 1 size single-bladed spinners or ⅛- to ¼-ounce crank baits. In early spring minnows are the most effective. Mid-June to mid-August crawfish are the best choice. Late summer and early fall, minnows and minnow lures are again popular. Natural baits such as crawfish, minnows, and worms can trigger a response when nothing else will. The meat is a cross between crappie and large-mouth bass, mild tasting, white, flaky, and low in oil content. Smallmouth bass can be cooked whole, but fillets are preferred.

Harold paddles the Cossatot River (Arkansas).

Smallmouth Bass with Bacon and Mushrooms

6 smallmouth bass fillets
1 quart ginger ale
8 pieces bacon
½ red onion, 1-inch slices
1 cup sliced portobello or mushroom caps
8 tablespoons butter
¼ teaspoon dried tarragon leaves
Paprika

Soak bass fillets in ginger ale overnight. Cook bacon and save drippings. Crumble bacon and set aside. Sauté onions and mushrooms in drippings until just tender. Place bass in a baking dish. Combine onion and mushroom mixture, butter, and tarragon; spread on top of fillets. Bake at 350° about 20 minutes or until fish flakes. Place on serving plates and sprinkle with bits of bacon.

Gingered Grilled Smallmouth Bass

1 small zucchini, thin strips
1 small yellow squash, thin strips
1 small carrot, thin strips
1 tablespoon fresh ginger, minced
4 smallmouth bass fillets
½ lemon
1 garlic clove, minced
White pepper to taste

Bring outdoor grill to medium heat. Cut four 16x16-inch pieces of foil, fold in half for double thickness. Mix zucchini, squash, carrots, and ginger. Divide into 4 portions and place on each foil piece. Top each with a bass fillet and sprinkle with lemon juice, garlic, and pepper. Fold foil and crimp edges to seal. Grill 15 to 20 minutes over medium heat or coals. Turn once. Serves 4.

The Long Walk with Jake

Jake was Everett Jr.'s favorite quail dog. I never quail hunted with Everett Jr., as he was all grown up and I was too young to manage the long walks through briars and tall grass. But I didn't need to go along in order to enjoy the hunts, because I spent many hours, over many seasons, riding with Everett in his old gray pick-up truck listening to stories about how he, Jake, and "Dog" Owens, the local high school football coach, would spend their Saturdays "huntin' bob white quail." The hair would stand up on the back of my neck each time Everett told me about the loud "fllrruuuuu" sound made when Jake missed a covey and they rose up behind them. I would sit there and in my minds eye I could see the four of us walking through fields of dry grass and I could see myself watching Jake standing frozen on a point, with his right front leg lifted, and his tail sticking straight out. I never thought about how many miles they had walked together over the years. It must have been substantial. When you are very young, you are never really aware of when some things begin or when they end. I was well out of college when I realized that it had been many years since Everett Jr. had spoken about ol' Jake and I could never bring myself to ask.

Quail in Brown Gravy

8 quail, split and flattened
½ teaspoon salt
¼ teaspoon pepper
¼ cup butter
1 chicken bouillon cube
1 cup boiling water
2 tablespoons flour
Mashed potatoes or cooked rice or noodles for four

Season quail with salt and pepper. Melt butter and brown quail on both sides. Dissolve bouillon cube in boiling water and add to quail. Cover and simmer 40 minutes. Remove quail. Add enough water to pan drippings to make one cup. Mix flour with 2 tablespoons water and gradually stir into drippings. Cook and stir over low heat until thickened. Add quail to gravy and heat. Serve with mashed potatoes, rice or noodles. Serves 4.

Crockpot Quail

8 cleaned quail, halved
Salt and pepper
1 cup flour
½ cup olive oil
2 cans chicken broth
½ cup white wine or grape juice
2 cans cream of celery soup
2 cans cream of chicken soup
½ onion, quartered
2 bay leaves
⅓ cup grated Parmesan cheese
Cooked rice or noodles for 4 to 6

Sprinkle quail with salt and pepper and coat with flour. Brown in oil. Place quail, broth, wine, soups, onion, and bay leaves in a crockpot and cook 4 hours on high. Reduce and cook 7 hours on low. Add cheese and cook another 30 minutes. Serve over rice or noodles. Serves 4 to 6.

Quail and Mushroom Casserole

12 quail breasts
5 tablespoons butter, divided
1 (16-ounce) can cream of chicken soup
1 tablespoon butter
¼ cup milk
¼ cup thinly sliced mushrooms
Salt and pepper

Preheat oven to 300°. Dip breasts in 4 tablespoons melted butter and brown in a casserole dish in the oven. Combine soup, remaining 1 tablespoon melted butter, milk, and mushrooms; pour over breasts. Season to taste. Bake 45 to 60 minutes. Serves 4.

Wild Quail in Plum Sauce

2 tablespoons butter, softened
⅓ cup plum jam
¼ teaspoon dried basil leaves (1 teaspoon fresh)
1 tablespoon red wine vinegar
12 quail, cleaned and flattened
Salt and pepper

Mix butter, jam, and basil. Melt over low heat and stir in vinegar. Place quail on grill, skin side down; turn and cook on both sides, 8 to 10 minutes total. During final 5 minutes, baste with jam sauce. Salt and pepper to taste. Serves 6.

Winter

Brer Rabbit and Da Stew Pot

Beagles are good rabbit dogs because both beagles and rabbits run around in circles. That is what my Uncle Everett once told me when I asked him why he always hunted rabbits with beagles. The truth is, rabbits run in circles and beagles follow. Beagles follow a scent trail and will search the densest of brier patches. All seasoned rabbit hunters know that when a rabbit is jumped, all they need to do is stand on the highest ground and watch the clearings ahead of the dogs. As long as the rabbit does not go down a hole, the beagles will keep it circling around. If you miss a shot, stay where you are, the rabbit will probably circle back around. Don't look at the dog. The dog is where the rabbit was and not where the rabbit is.

Tender Rabbit

1 rabbit, serving-size pieces
1 quart vinegar
2 tablespoons salt
1 tablespoon pickling spice
1 tablespoon whole peppercorns
2 large onions, sliced, divided
2 tablespoons bacon drippings
2 tablespoons flour in 1 cup cold water
1 teaspoon ground cinnamon
½ teaspoon ground allspice

Place rabbit, vinegar, spices, and 1 onion in a glass container. Cover and refrigerate 24 hours. Drain, cover with boiling water and simmer 1½ hours or until meat is tender. Melt fat in a skillet; add flour/water mixture, rabbit, strained broth, cinnamon, allspice and remaining onion. Simmer 1 hour.

Stewed Rabbit

½ cup flour
½ teaspoon salt
¼ teaspoon pepper
2 to 3 pounds rabbit, serving-size pieces
6 slices bacon, halved
1 bell pepper, chopped
2 tomatoes, quartered
1 large onion, quartered
2 medium carrots, cut 2-inches long
2 garlic cloves, minced
1 bay leaf, halved
1¼ cups water
¾ cup dry red wine or grape juice
1 tablespoon packed, dark brown sugar
½ teaspoon salt
½ teaspoon rosemary leaves
½ teaspoon paprika
1 tablespoon cornstarch
2 tablespoons cold water

Mix flour, salt and pepper; dredge rabbit pieces. Cook bacon until crisp, drain and crumble. Place 3 tablespoons bacon grease into a large pot and brown rabbit on all sides. Add remaining ingredients except cornstarch and water. Heat to boiling, reduce heat, cover and simmer 1 to 1½ hours or until rabbit is tender. Remove rabbit and vegetables. Mix cornstarch with water, stir into pot liquid and heat until thickens. Pour over rabbit and vegetables. Serves 6.

Baked Rabbit

2 small rabbits, serving-size pieces
Flour seasoned with salt and pepper
3 tablespoons bacon drippings
1 large onion, sliced
¼ teaspoon each thyme, pepper, salt
1 cup sour cream

Dredge rabbit pieces in seasoned flour. Heat drippings in an oven-proof casserole dish and brown rabbit on all sides. Layer with onions, seasonings, and sour cream. Cover and bake at 300° for 1 hour.

Fried Rabbit with Gravy

⅓ cup plus 3 tablespoons flour, divided
Salt and pepper
1 rabbit, serving-size pieces
Vegetable oil
1½ cups milk

Combine ⅓ cup flour and salt and pepper to taste; dredge rabbit pieces. Heat ¼-inch oil in a skillet and brown rabbit on all sides. Reduce heat, cover and simmer 20 to 25 minutes or until tender. Remove rabbit to paper towels to drain. Save 3 tablespoons oil, stir in 3 tablespoons flour, blend in milk, and cook over medium heat until thickened. Salt and pepper to taste.

I Wish I Were a Wing Shot

I don't mind standing in the dark and trembling in freezing cold water. Well I really do mind it, but I would mind it much less if I were a fair wing shot — which I am not. This story goes back more than fifty years to the time that my father gave me a shotgun with a long, full-choked barrel. I just assumed that one shotgun was as good as another and would serve just as well for duck as it did for deer. As a result, my formative duck hunting years did very little to teach me the proper wing shooting techniques. That Winchester Model 12 is now archived in the back of my gun safe and a Browning A5 with interchangeable chokes has taken its place. I get a duck every now and then but nothing like my friends. The folks I hunt with don't rag me much about my being a poor shot. I suppose this is because if they ragged me very much, I may not come back and one of them would have to do the cooking.

Apple-Stewed Duck

2 ducks, sectioned
1 apple, peeled, cored and quartered
1 potato, peeled and quartered
Bacon grease
Salt and pepper
1 cup water
Cornmeal
Milk

Mix and place first five ingredients in a deep casserole dish. Add water. Cover and simmer until duck is tender. Discard apple and potato. Mix cornmeal with a little milk, pat into dumplings and place on top of duck. Bake uncovered at 350° until done. Serves 4.

Fried Duck Parmesan

2 duck breasts, sliced
1 egg beaten with 1 teaspoon water
¼ cup grated Parmesan cheese
1 cup olive oil

Dip breasts in egg and then roll in cheese. Heat olive oil in a skillet and sauté breasts until golden and just beginning to firm. Serves 2.

Duck Liver and Apricot Sauce

2 ½ cups canned apricots, drained
1 tablespoon orange zest
2 cups red wine
2 tablespoons butter, softened
Salt and pepper
2 to 4 cooked duck livers, puréed

Purée apricots, mix in orange zest, wine, butter, and salt and pepper to taste. Bring to a boil. Mix in duck livers, reduce heat and simmer 5 minutes. Serve as a sauce over duck or geese. Serves 4 to 6.

Orange-Baked Duck

1 cup warm water
2 tablespoons orange marmalade
1 can unfrozen orange juice concentrate
1 package brown gravy mix
2 tablespoons sugar
¼ cup flour
1 teaspoon salt
2 mallard duck or 1 small goose

Preheat oven to 375°. Mix all ingredients except duck and place in a large plastic roasting bag; add ducks and coat with mixture. Seal bag, place in a deep roasting pan, and make several small cuts in top of bag. Bake ducks 1½ to 2 hours or until tender. Cut duck in half before serving. Reserve liquid and use for a sauce. Serves 4.

Spicy Duck Sausage Mold

2 pounds ground duck
4 ounces boneless pork chops
2 tablespoons salt
1 teaspoon red pepper flakes (optional)
1 tablespoon toasted coriander seed
½ teaspoon toasted cumin seed
½ teaspoon black pepper
1 tablespoon sugar
½ cup port wine
½ cup shaved or crushed ice

Mix all ingredients except port and ice; chill then grind. Set aside ¼ of the mixture. Process the remainder and slowly add wine and enough water to make thick paste; mix with remaining duck. Press into a mold, cover and freeze. To serve, slice and sauté. Serves 6.

Targeting the Walleye

Walleye originally inhabited waters in the northern U.S. and Canada. Growing up in the south, I had never heard of "Old Marble-Eyes." Walleye has grown in popularity in the south since it was introduced into our large reservoirs and the stockings have been extremely successful. Walleye feed primarily during the low-light periods at dawn and dusk. Favorite feeding locations are around rocks, structures, and the edge of weed beds where they feed on crawfish and bait fish. Chartreuse crawfish patterns work well in very deep water and lighter colors work best in clear water. Shad Raps and Storm Deep Thunder Sticks are favorite crank baits. If you will add a length of night crawler to the treble hooks, you will sometimes give the fish exactly what they want. The first time I ever heard of Walleye was the Summer of 1971 when I was teaching a class in Mt. Home, Arkansas. Some of the guys in the class were talking about how they SCUBA fished in Beaver Lake for Walleye and one of the guys was gracious enough to invite me over for dinner featuring some of his catches. Walleye is a very meaty, fine-flaked, and practically sweet-flavored fish. The preferred cooking methods are poaching or baking, but it may also be pan-fried, deep-fried and broiled.

Spear fishing off
Cancun in Winter.

Walleye Sauté

1 pound walleye fillets
2 tablespoons vegetable oil
1 cup sliced onions
1 cup julienned carrots
1 large bell pepper, julienned
2 large tomatoes, peeled and wedged
½ teaspoon chopped, fresh basil
Salt and pepper

Cut fillets into bite-size pieces. Heat oil in a skillet and add onions, carrots, and bell pepper. Sauté 10 minutes or until vegetables are just tender. Add walleye and remaining ingredients, cover, reduce heat to simmer and cook 10 minutes or until flesh is flaky. Serves 6.

Baked Walleye Oriental

1 tablespoon lemon zest
½ cup lemon juice
¼ cup sherry, white wine or water
3 tablespoons vegetable oil
2 tablespoons soy sauce
¼ tablespoon black pepper
¼ cup diced green onion
1 tablespoon shredded fresh ginger
4 walleye fillets

Combine ingredients in glass dish, add fillet, cover and refrigerate 6 hours. Remove fish (discard marinade) and bake 20 minutes at 350° or until flesh is firm. Serves 6.

Walleye Chowder

8 slices bacon, chopped
2 small onions, finely chopped
2 carrots, finely chopped
2 celery ribs, finely chopped
4 tablespoons unsalted butter
4 teaspoons all-purpose flour
1 teaspoon paprika
1 (16-ounce) bottle clam juice
2 cups water
1 cup cream
1 pound potatoes
1½ pounds walleye, 1-inch pieces
3 tablespoons minced, fresh parsley
Salt and pepper

Fry bacon until crisp; drain. Add onion, carrot, celery, and butter to skillet; sauté over medium heat until just soft. Sprinkle with flour and cook 3 minutes. Add paprika, clam juice, water, and cream; bring to a boil. Stir. In a separate pot, boil potatoes until peel loosens; peel, cut into ½-inch cubes and add to chowder. Simmer uncovered 15 minutes or until potatoes are cooked. Add fish and simmer 5 minutes. Add parsley and season to taste. Serves 4.

Italian-Fried Walleye

1 cup Parmesan cheese
2 cups Italian-flavored breadcrumbs
3 pounds walleye fillets, skinned
Peanut oil

Dip fish in a mixture of cheese and breadcrumbs. Fry in oil until golden. Serves 4 to 6.

Fresh Frozen Rabbit To Go

For the record, rabbit does look and taste like chicken. I like chicken just about any way you cook it. Since I discovered that my supermarket carried domestic rabbit, it has been on my menu at least four times a year. Rabbit is a little more expensive than chicken, but it is much less expensive than beef. When I first found rabbit in the grocery cooler, I was a little hesitant to purchase it so I copied down the name of the rabbit farm, gave them a call, and scheduled a visit. The owner told me how he raises and processes his rabbits, but I wanted to see for myself. It was a first-class operation and clean as could be. I was led into the packaging room, and it was equipped better than many grocery store meat markets I have visited. Now I frequently enjoy fresh, frozen rabbit "to go."

Sweet and Sour Rabbit

¾ **cup flour**
Salt and pepper
2½ **pounds rabbit, sectioned**
2 **tablespoons oil**
¼ **cup rice wine or white vinegar**
1 **cup pineapple juice**
1 **green bell pepper, sliced**
1 **cup pineapple chunks**
1½ **tablespoons cornstarch**
½ **cup water**
¼ **cup sugar**

Sift flour with salt and pepper to taste; dredge rabbit. Brown in heated oil. Add vinegar, pineapple juice, and ½ teapoon salt. Cover and simmer until rabbit is tender, about 40 minutes. Add bell pepper and pineapple chunks; cover and cook until peppers wilt. Whisk cornstarch into water and slowly stir into rabbit. Mix in sugar. Stir-cook 5 minutes. Serves 4.

Grilled Rabbit Rolls

3½ pounds rabbit
Salt and pepper
3 tablespoons minced fresh parsley
2 tablespoons minced fresh rosemary
¼ pound ham, sliced thin
6 skewers
12 sage leaves
6 (¾-inch) pieces Italian sausage
½ cup olive oil

Bone rabbit; cut into 12 pieces, flatten out and season with salt and pepper to taste. Sprinkle with parsley and rosemary. Place a slice of ham on top and roll tightly. Skewer a rabbit roll, a sage leaf, 1 sausage slice, another sage leaf, and another rabbit roll. Repeat with each skewer. Coat with olive oil and grill basting with olive oil. Serves 6.

Baked Rabbit and Cabbage

1 cabbage, shredded
4 green onions, sliced
2 celery stalks, sliced
3 carrots, sliced
11 ounces ham, chopped
3 garlic cloves, minced
1 rabbit, sectioned
1 teaspoon minced fresh thyme
2 bay leaves
2 sprigs fresh parsley, chopped
½ cup water
Salt and pepper

Preheat oven to 350°. Mix cabbage, green onions, celery, carrots, ham, and garlic. Place ½ on bottom of casserole dish. Add rabbit and sprinkle with thyme, bay leaves, and parsley. Top with remaining cabbage mixture. Pour in water and season with salt and pepper to taste. Cover and bake 2 hours. Serves 4.

Rabbit Casserole

2 pounds rabbit, sectioned
1 onion, sliced
1 tablespoon oil
1 tablespoon butter, softened
½ tomato, puréed
2 celery stalks, chopped
1 tablespoon capers, drained
1 tablespoon sugar
½ cup red wine
1 cup beef or chicken broth
Salt, pepper, and thyme
1 tablespoon flour
¼ cup water

Preheat oven to 350°. Place rabbit in a casserole dish. Sauté onion in oil and butter; add to casserole dish. Mix in tomato, celery, capers, sugar, wine, broth, and seasonings. Cover and bake 1½ hours. Whisk flour into water, stir into casserole and bake 15 minutes. Serves 4.

Swamp hunting with J. and Mr. Will.

T-Bones and Mashed Potatoes

I was on a 10-day mule deer hunting trip in Wells, Nevada, when I accidentally broke-out of the Venison Summer Sausage and Venison Bacon-Burger mold. Two of us were lucky enough to have filled our mule deer tags. After watching my deer hang in the naturally cool root cellar for several days, I noticed a meat saw hanging on the wall and my mouth began to water. Our guide saw me looking at the saw and the deer and she suggested that we have broiled venison T-bone steaks for dinner. I had never associated T-bone steaks with venison and I had always been told that you couldn't broil venison. I learned a lot that day. We disjointed and dropped the hindquarters; cut the saddle off behind the last rib, sawed down the middle of the saddle, and from each side we cut off beautiful 1¼-inch-thick T-bone steaks. Susan broiled some of the best venison steaks I have ever put in my mouth. If you are planning on broiling bone-in or loin steaks the two tricks are: (1) Cut the steaks between 1- to 1¼-inches thick and (2) Cook them to no more than medium-rare (138-degree internal temperature).

Broiled Venison T-Bone Steaks

8 venison T-bone steaks, 1-inch thick
1 onion, sliced
1 green bell pepper, sliced
Olive or other cooking oil
Salt and pepper

Place steaks with onion and bell pepper rings in a large zip-lock bag; cover with olive oil. Place in refrigerator 30 minutes. Remove and sprinkle both sides with salt and pepper. Place on a broiler rack and cook on one side until the high points just begin to brown. Turn over and repeat. Cook until surface just begins to firm. Do not over-cook. While steak is cooking, sauté vegetables until tender. Plate steak; cover with vegetables. Serves 4.

Grilled Venison T-Bone Steaks with Bourbon Marinade

Bourbon Marinade:

4 cups sour mash bourbon
¼ cup salad oil
2 tablespoons teriyaki or soy sauce
1 teaspoon Worcestershire sauce
2 cloves garlic, minced
¼ teaspoon black pepper

Grilled Venison T-bone Steaks:

4 venison T-bone steaks, 1½- to 2-inches thick
2 tablespoons butter
¼ cup chopped onion
¼ cup chopped green bell pepper
½ cup chopped celery
1 (8-ounce) can unseasoned tomatoes
½ teaspoon sugar
⅛ teaspoon garlic powder
Salt and pepper
Dijon or other French-style mustard

To make Bourbon Marinade, combine all ingredients in 1 gallon resealable plastic bag. Mix well and add venison steaks. Refrigerate 4 to 6 hours to marinate steaks. To cook steaks, remove from marinade and set aside to drain. In a saucepan, melt butter; add onion, bell pepper, and celery. Cook only until onion turns just clear and set aside. Drain tomatoes, reserving liquid, and chop. Add chopped tomatoes and reserved juice to vegetables. Cook 5 minutes over low heat. Add sugar and garlic powder. Season with salt and pepper to taste and simmer 10 minutes. Brush steaks lightly with mustard and season with salt and pepper to taste. Grill 5 to 6 minutes per side. Do not over-cook. Steaks should be cooked to rare or no more than medium rare. To serve, spoon some onion-tomato sauce on the center of each serving plate and lay on a venison steak. Serves 4.

Venison Béarnaise

4 slices venison loin, 2-inches thick
¼ cup Worcestershire sauce
Salt and pepper
Instant béarnaise Sauce, prepared
Paprika
Parsley sprigs

Place venison and Worcestershire sauce in a plastic bag and refrigerate 1 hour. Grill both sides until just medium (138°). Plate and cover with béarnaise sauce; garnish with paprika and parsley sprigs. Serve with Mashed Potatoes Royale. Serves 4.

Mashed Potatoes Royale

2½ pounds whole potatoes
1 pound whole onions
1¼ cups cream
8 tablespoons real salted butter, melted
1½ tablespoons chopped fresh parsley
¼ teaspoon fresh grated nutmeg
¼ teaspoon white pepper
¼ teaspoon salt

Boil potatoes and onions together until tender. Peel potatoes and pass through a potato ricer or mash until only very small lumps remain. Place in electric mixing bowl. Peel and chop onions and add to potatoes. Turn mixer on slow and add remaining ingredients. Serves 8.

More than One Way to Eat an Oyster

Americans probably eat more oysters than anyone else in the world and there are several reasons why. Fresh-shucked oysters now appear in the supermarket twelve months of the year and oysters can be prepared in so many different ways. There are few food items that can be eaten raw, made into a soup, broiled, roasted, grilled, stewed, sautéed, barbequed, or any other way you wish. My two favorite ways to eat oysters are either cold and raw with a horseradish-ketchup-Tabasco sauce and a twist of lemon or hot oyster soup with a grind of fresh nutmeg on top. The trick to cooking perfect oysters is not to over-cook them. In soups, stews and gumbo add the oysters during the last five minutes of cooking. In the broiler, on the grill or in the oven, cook only until the outer edges begin to curl. As with most seafood, when oysters are over-cooked, they begin to toughen. The coastal oyster beds are so regulated and frequently tested that there is no longer a need to worry about getting bad oysters than there is to worry about getting bad beef.

Puffed Oysters

1 cup water
½ cup butter
1 cup flour
¼ teaspoon salt
4 eggs
1¼ cups fresh oysters, drained
Cocktail sauce

Preheat oven to 400°. Heat water to a boil and add butter. Whisk in flour and salt. Reduce heat and stir until mixture makes a ball and pulls away from the side of the pot. Remove from heat and set aside. Beat in eggs, one at a time, until smooth and stir in oysters. Spoon up dough with one oyster and place on an ungreased baking sheet; repeat using all dough. Bake 25 minutes or until puffed and golden brown. Serve with cocktail sauce.

Creamed Oyster Soup

4 tablespoons butter, divided
2 tablespoons chili sauce
2 tablespoons Worcestershire sauce
½ cup oyster liquid
1 teaspoon Paprika
¼ teaspoon celery salt
2 ounces clam juice
16 fresh oysters
1 cup cream
2 slices toast
Nutmeg

In a double boiler, melt 2 tablespoons butter and add remaining ingredients, except cream and toast. Cook and gently whisk until oyster edges begin to curl. Add cream and whisk. Place toast in individual bowls and cover with oyster soup. Garnish with remaining butter and a sprinkling of nutmeg. Serves 2.

Smoked Oyster Bisque

2 tablespoons butter, softened
⅓ cup minced onion
8 ounces smoked oysters, drained
½ cup white wine
½ teaspoon chopped fresh thyme
2 teaspoons minced fresh parsley
1 cup cream
Salt and pepper

Melt butter and sauté onions until just clear. Stir in remaining ingredients except cream and salt and pepper; bring just to a boil. Stir in cream and season to taste with salt and pepper. Serves 2.

Christmas Fishing in Ixtapa

A week before Christmas 1982, I had a job that was eating me alive. I needed a break. I went by a travel agents office and asked, "What's popular this time of year?" "Ixtapa," she said. "My lord, Ixtapa!" The memories flashed through my brain just like it was yesterday. It had been fifteen years since I was a flower child traveling through Mexico and accidentally finding Ixtapa.

The summer of 1967 was an interesting time for an adventurous 22 year old. I had started driving south and eventually found myself in Acapulco and was told about the sleepy fishing village of Zihuatanejo. On the other side of the mountain was the tiny settlement of Ixtapa. The village of Ixtapa, if you can even call it a village, was situated on the beach and nestled amongst miles of coconut plantation. It was here that I spent the remainder of the summer sleeping in my tent on a beach and savoring life.

Harold walking the beach of Ixtapa in 1967.

So 15 years later, I booked a flight to Zihuatanejo and a room in the Ixtapa Holiday Inn. The Holiday Inn should have gotten my attention. The village of Zihuatanejo had changed very little; it was still as quaint as I remembered it. But where did all the tourists come from? When the taxi passed over the hill and dropped me off at my hotel in Ixtapa nothing was as I remembered it—everywhere were high-rise hotels, fast-food restaurants, and bikinis with children in tow.

I migrated back over the hill to Zihuatanejo, where the old fishing boats once docked, and asked a captain for permission to come aboard one of the new charter fishing boats. I asked the skipper if he was planning on working Christmas Eve. He said, "No. But would you like to go fishing?" "Of course. How much?" "Gas plus $50.00 US and you catch fish or you won't owe the $50.00," he said. On Christmas Eve we went out and within ten minutes the cloths-pin had popped and I was on the sailfish ride of my life. My skipper offered to send it off to Mexico City and have it mounted for me and asked me if he could have the meat. "I have a large family and it will be our Christmas dinner tomorrow," he said. "What are you going to do with the $50.00?" I inquired. "This is Christmas Eve and I don't work on Christmas Eve. At midnight mass tonight, I will put your money for you in the box for the poor."

Sailfish and Onion Steak

1 large onion, sliced
1 tablespoon butter
1 teaspoon olive oil
1 tablespoon minced fresh thyme
1 tablespoon minced fresh oregano
1 pound sail or swordfish steaks
Salt and pepper
Flour
1 tablespoon chopped fresh parsley
¼ cup breadcrumbs
⅓ cup white wine

Sauté onions in butter and olive oil until just clear; stir in thyme and oregano. Remove onions, and set aside. Season fish with salt and pepper to taste; dredge in flour. Brown steaks on both sides. Place fish in a large casserole dish; cover with onions. Mix parsley into breadcrumbs and sprinkle over onions. Pour wine around dish and bake 25 to 35 minutes until breadcrumbs begin to brown. Serves 2.

Fifteen years later
— Ixtapa, Christmas 1982.

Simply Grilled Sailfish

¼ cup fresh lemon juice, strained
¼ cup white wine
Salt and pepper
4 sail or swordfish steaks

Mix all ingredients and marinate fish 2 hours in refrigerator. Grill 4 minutes per side until just firm. Serves 4.

Broiled Sailfish Piccata

½ teaspoon pepper
1 pound sail or swordfish, ½-inch thick
1 tablespoon minced fresh parsley
2 teaspoons minced fresh cilantro
2 tablespoons fresh lemon juice, strained
2 teaspoons capers
Lemon slices

Pepper fish and place on a broiler pan; broil 1½ minutes each side until flesh begins to firm. Place on serving plates and sprinkle with parsley, cilantro, lemon juice and capers. Serve with lemon slices. Serves 4.

Elegant Christmas Goose

The typical centerpiece at an 1800's Christmas dinner would have been a wild goose with a wild rice stuffing, a sweet potato soufflé, Cumberland sauce, and all the other trimmings that go along with this festive season. The principle goose harvested in the United States is the Canada goose and depending on the race, it will weigh between 3 and 20 pounds. One normally does not roast birds weighing more than 10 pounds. Young geese may be roasted; older birds will be too tough and will have to wait for the stew pot. Even young birds may have a tendency to be tough and dry. There are four things, which you can do to minimize the dryness and toughness: (1) Inject melted butter into the breasts and legs, (2) Cook the bird very slowly and baste while cooking, (3) Cook to no more than rare or medium rare, and (4) Carve the bird into thin-sliced servings.

Roasted Wild Canada Goose

½ pound butter melted
1 goose
Wild Rice Stuffing (see recipe page 201)

Inject melted butter deep into each breast, leg, and thigh. Stuff goose with Wild Rice Stuffing and seal the cavity. Place goose on a pan with a raised rack. Fill the pan with ¾-inch water. Water may need to be replenished during cooking. Set oven at 350°. Insert a meat thermometer deep into the thigh, being careful to not touch the bone. Cook to 140°. Remove and cover with aluminum foil and allow to rest 15 minutes. Serve with Sweet Potato Soufflé.

Wild Rice Stuffing

1 cup uncooked wild rice
1 cup sliced mushrooms
8 tablespoons butter, melted
1 bunch green onions, minced
¾ cup chopped celery
1 garlic clove, minced
¼ cup minced parsley
Salt and pepper

Cook rice according to directions on package. Sauté mushrooms in butter until limp, about 5 minutes. Remove mushrooms and set aside. Add onions and celery and cook about 8 minutes. Stir in garlic, parsley, cooked wild rice, mushrooms, and salt and pepper to taste.

Sweet Potato Soufflé

2 cups cooked sweet potatoes, mashed
1½ cups sugar
2 eggs beaten
½ cup milk
8 tablespoons butter, softened, divided
½ teaspoon ground cinnamon
½ teaspoon ground nutmeg
6 tablespoons butter, divided
½ cup Rice Krispies
½ cup chopped pecans
½ cup packed brown sugar

Preheat oven to 350°. Combine and mix well the sweet potatoes, sugar, eggs, milk, 2 tablespoons butter, and seasonings. Spoon into 10-inch buttered casserole. Combine Rice Krispies, pecans, remaining 6 tablespoons butter, and brown sugar; mix until crumbly. Sprinkle over sweet potato mixture and bake 20 minutes. Serves 6.

Cumberland Sauce

2 oranges
2 lemons
¼ teaspoon maraschino cherry juice
½ cup currant jelly
1 cup port wine
1 tablespoon arrowroot
1 tablespoon water

Peel the rind of 1 orange and 1 lemon. Shred and set aside. Squeeze the juice from lemons and oranges and strain; add cherry juice and combine with jelly in a saucepan. Bring to a slow boil and simmer 3 minutes; add port wine. Stir arrowroot into water until smooth. Stir into the boiling liquid. Cook a few minutes until sauce has thickened slightly. Add rind. Sauce improves if made the day ahead and reheated.

Spreading Out the New Year's Party

Over the years and at my age, the New Year's party has progressed steadily downward; from dancing, beer, and pickled eggs at Bubba's Road House, to a gathering of close friends—not so much to celebrate the new year, as it is to celebrate making it through another one. Pickled eggs still appear on the menu, but the beer has given way to Diet Coke. The remainder of the food has taken on an image more in keeping with my grey hair and my more sedate lifestyle. Everyone always wants to know what we are having to eat, so I have taken to framing and posting the menu on the wall. I prefer to serve a large quantity of three or four simple cold appetizers that can be made the day before and one hot and fancy appetizer when midnight finally arrives. In keeping with the spirit of the moment, magnums of champagne have also given way to cold bottles of sparkling white grape juice.

Seasoned Bass Dip

2 cups cooked bass fillets
1 cup cottage cheese
¾ cup sour cream
2 tablespoons chicken broth
1 tablespoon chopped pimento
1 tablespoon minced fresh parsley
Salt and white pepper
Chopped parsley

Combine all ingredients, except chopped parsley, cover and refrigerate for 2 hours. Garnish with chopped parsley. Serve with crackers or chips.

Oyster and Mushroom Dip

¼ cup flour
¼ cup cooking oil
4 green onions, minced
2 celery stalks, minced
1½ pounds small mushrooms, de-stemmed
24 fresh oysters, drained
½ cup oyster liquid
1 garlic clove, minced
1 teaspoon minced fresh parsley
½ teaspoon white pepper
½ teaspoon salt

Mix flour and oil in a skillet and stir over medium heat until light brown. Mix in green onions and celery; simmer until celery is tender. Add remaining ingredients; gently simmer until mushrooms wilt and sauce thickens. Serve with vegetables or chips for dipping.

Spicy Crab and Egg Dip

1 cup crabmeat, drained
1 hard-boiled egg, chopped
½ cup chili sauce
½ teaspoon Tabasco sauce
½ teaspoon Worcestershire sauce
½ cup real mayonnaise
1 garlic clove, minced
½ teaspoon salt

Combine, cover, and refrigerate overnight. Place dip in a bowl and serve with assorted crackers.

Shrimp Cocktail Sauce

2 cups mayonnaise
1 teaspoon minced capers
1 teaspoon minced anchovies
Juice of ½ lemon, strained
⅛ teaspoon Tabasco sauce
⅛ teaspoon Worcestershire sauce
1 dill pickle, minced
½ cup minced parsley
2 teaspoons prepared horseradish
2 tablespoons Dijon mustard
1 garlic clove, minced
2 tablespoons minced onion
1½ pounds shrimp, boiled, shelled
1 head lettuce, shredded

Stir together all ingredients except shrimp and lettuce; cover and refrigerate overnight. Serve shrimp on a bed of lettuce and cover with sauce.

Typhoon Russ
and New Year's Eve on Guam

The island of Guam is a United States South Pacific territory located near Micronesia in the southwest Pacific about 500 miles north of the Equator. I arrived on the island between Christmas and New Years, one day after the worst typhoon (hurricane) in the last fifty years. As far as hurricanes go this had been a bad one, but in the south pacific large hurricanes are a way of life. Commercial buildings are built to stand up to the massive winds, but residences don't seem to fall under any building codes. As in most natural disasters, it is the homes that receive the most damage. Guamanians are a resilient people. My work was difficult at best, but during this time, I became a close and personal friend to several local co-workers. As I was closing the office on New Year's Eve one of my new friends came over and invited me to a New Year's party at his home. As with all small islands, Guam is dependent on a steady supply of ship-born goods for everything from milk to bed linens. I knew that there was only a ten-day food supply on the island and wondered how a party could be given when basic staples were in short supply. My treat was a party that featured traditional food and traditional recipes, some a thousand years old that were made from the bounty of the island. I insisted that I be allowed to participate not only in the festivities, but also in the preparation of the food. Because there was no electrical power except for generators, the party finally broke up at 2:00 am when the last candle burned out. There may have been only a ten-day supply of food on the island, but there was a ten-year supply of Fosters Australian beer. When the island got down to a two-day supply of meat, instead of going to the market, my hosts would invite me down to the sea where they taught me to catch reef fish with casting nets. We would ride water buffalos into the hills to harvest coconuts that had fallen during the storm. Coconut is a staple of the pacific islanders diet. I ate coconut prepared in so many different ways that it was some years before I could look another coconut straight in the eyes.

Clam Kelaguen

1 package fresh clams
2 green onions, chopped
2 cayenne peppers, chopped (optional)
1 teaspoon salt
Juice of 2 lemons
½ fresh coconut, grated
Cooked rice or flour tortillas for 4

Wash clam meat and chop into small pieces. Mix together onions, peppers, salt and lemon juice. Pour onion-lemon mixture over clams and mix well. Cover and place in refrigerator for 1 hour. Mix in coconut and serve with flour tortillas or cooked rice. Serves 4.

Coconut Candy

3 cups sugar
1 cup milk
3 cups fresh shredded coconut

Place sugar and milk in a saucepan and cook over medium heat until it makes a thin syrup (232° to 240° on a candy thermometer). Mix in coconut; stir constantly until golden brown. Remove from heat and spread onto a flat dish. Allow to cool before breaking into pieces. Makes 24 servings.

Riding a
water buffalo in Guam.

Portable Feasts

Whether it is a celebration on New Year's Eve or a football feast, appetizers are the perfect way to celebrate the successes of your fall harvest and show off your creative culinary skills. Above all else, appetizers should be attractive, easy to make, easy to transport, and simple to serve. They should be firm and easily managed on paper plate and with plastic utensils. Appetizers that require being served as soon as done are doomed to failure. I once served delicious Baked Oysters on the Half shell with a Champagne-Cheese Sauce at a Super Bowl party. Never again. Those who sampled them as soon as they came out of the oven raved. Those who waited until half time were disappointed. Prime candidates are: seafood dips, easily warmed fried platters, and refrigerated dishes. Poor candidates are anything that is broiled, is fluid and moves around on the plate, or must be eaten hot off the stove or with a spoon.

Dove Appetizers

Dove breasts
Worcestershire sauce
Bacon strips
Toothpicks, uncolored
Salt and white pepper to taste
Parsley sprigs for garnish

Dip breasts in Worcestershire sauce and set in refrigerator for 15 minutes. Wrap breasts in bacon and secure with toothpick. Sprinkle with salt and pepper. Grill, broil, or sauté until bacon begins to crisp and juices run clear. Garnish with parsley.

Venison Sausage and Cheese Dip

1 pound Velveeta cheese
1 can chili without beans
1 pound venison sausage, cooked and crumbled
Salted tortilla chips

Melt cheese; mix in chili and sausage. Serve from a fondue or small crock-pot with salted tortilla chips for dipping. Recipe can be doubled.

Fried Catfish Fingers with Spicy Dipping Sauce

Fish:

Peanut oil for frying
2 cups white cornmeal
Salt and pepper
2½ pounds catfish fillets, 1-inch wide strips

Dipping Sauce:

¾ cup white wine vinegar
½ teaspoon salt
½ teaspoon pepper
1 small white onion, minced
2 garlic cloves, minced
2 green onions, sliced thin
1 tablespoon minced fresh parsley

Heat oil to 375°. Mix cornmeal, salt and pepper and dredge fillets. Fry a few fillets at a time until golden; drain. Sprinkle lightly with salt. Fish can be refrigerated and warmed at a later date. Just before serving, prepare dipping sauce by whisking remaining ingredients in a bowl.

Crab and Spinach Dip

½ medium onion, finely chopped
½ cup butter, melted
1 (7-ounce) can crabmeat
¾ cup Parmesan cheese
1 package frozen spinach, cooked
Ritz crackers

Add onion to melted butter and sauté until soft. Add crabmeat and cheese. Cook until cheese is melted; add spinach. Serve from a chaffing dish with Ritz crackers.

Oyster Spread

1 teaspoon lemon juice
½ teaspoon Worcestershire sauce
1 tablespoon mayonnaise
1 (8-ounce) package cream cheese, softened
1 can smoked oysters, drained, chopped
Lightly salted crackers

Add lemon juice, Worcestershire sauce, and mayonnaise to cream cheese and blend until smooth. Stir in smoked oysters. Serve with crackers.

Backstrap or Tenderloin or Loin or Baby Tenderloin?

Depending on where you live, these choice parts of the deer go under different names. Backstrap, Loin, Tenderloin, and Baby Tenderloin are often confused with each other. In supermarket terms there are only two names: Loin and Tenderloin. The loins are the two long muscles which run along both sides of the backbone on the outside of the deer. The tenderloins are small and located on the inside of the body. No matter what you call these two muscles they are the choicest cuts and their price in the supermarket will verify their superiority in tenderness and taste. Depending on how a cow, pig, goat, sheep, or deer are butchered, these choice cuts appear under different guises and under different names. T-bone and porterhouse steaks contain parts of both. The large piece of meat in the T-bone is loin and the small piece is tenderloin. Chops and rib steaks are made from the loin after the tenderloin is used to make Filet Mignon.

Sautéed Venison Tenderloin with Mushroom Spaghetti

2 venison tenderloins
Salt and pepper
4 tablespoons bacon drippings
2 cans cream of mushroom soup
Cooked spaghetti for 6

Season tenderloins with salt and pepper. Sauté in drippings until they just begin to firm. Do not over-cook; set aside to rest. Warm soup. Slice tenderloins across the grain into ¼-inch-thin slices. Stir sliced tenderloins into soup, and serve over spaghetti. Serves 6.

Blue Cheese Venison Loin Steaks

1 ounce cream cheese, softened
2 tablespoons blue cheese, crumbled
4 teaspoons plain yogurt
2 teaspoons minced onion
⅛ teaspoon white pepper
2 pounds venison loin, cut from large end
1 garlic clove, crushed
Salt
2 teaspoons minced fresh parsley

Combine cheeses, yogurt, onion and pepper; set aside. Cut loin across the grain into 1-inch-thick pieces; rub with garlic. Place under the broiler and broil until the tips begin to brown. Season with salt; turn and broil on other side. Remove and season with salt to taste. Top each steak with cheese mixture and return to broiler for only a moment until just the tips of cheese begins to brown. Remove venison from broiler and sprinkle with parsley before serving. Serves 6.

Baked Venison Loin

3 pounds venison loin
Olive oil
3 teaspoons garlic salt
1½ teaspoons black pepper
White cotton string
4 slices bacon
1 stick butter

Coat loin with olive oil; rub in garlic salt and pepper. Tie loin every two inches with white cotton string. Insert a meat thermometer all the way into the large end. Place in a large baking pan, cover with bacon, and add butter. Place in a 350° oven and bake until thermometer reaches 138°. Remove; wrap in aluminum foil and allow to rest 10 minutes. Slice and serve. Serves 6.

Braided and Grilled Venison Tenderloin

3 venison tenderloins
2 (12-inch) skewers
1 cup teriyaki sauce
¼ cup olive oil
Salt and pepper

Cut two tenderloins long-ways beginning 1-inch from the large end and slice lengthwise. Slice the third tenderloin lengthwise all the way down and place one slice on the partially split tenderloin. Braid and skewer as you braid. Repeat with the other 1½ tenderloins. Marinate 1 hour in teriyaki sauce. Remove, wipe dry, and soak in olive oil 30 minutes. Season with salt and pepper. Place on a hot grill and cook until the meat just begins to firm. Serves 2.

Chasing the Schooling Winter Perch

White perch can be found all across the country. In the spring, schools of white perch, sometimes numbering in the thousands, leave the lakes on their annual migration to inlet coastal streams to reproduce. In the winter and early spring, they can be found in lakes, rivers, and reservoirs. At 8 ounces to 2 pounds, the white perch is no competition to the largemouth bass in size, but a child with a cane pole can make a memory that will last a lifetime. White perch prefer vegetated waters, with a firm bottom of sand or rock, and they completely avoid fast-moving water.

White Perch with Cherries and Cucumbers

1 cup pitted fresh cherries
3 cucumbers, peeled, cored, and sliced
1 cup water
4 tablespoons butter
Salt and pepper
4 white perch fillets

Place all ingredients, except perch, in a saucepan; cover and cook 4 minutes. Place perch in a buttered baking dish and cover with cherry cucumber mixture. Bake in a 300° oven for 20 minutes or until flesh is firm. Serves 8.

Simmered White Perch
with Mushroom and Lemon Sauce

3 cups sliced, fresh mushrooms
3 green onions, chopped
¼ cup plus 2 tablespoons butter, divided
1 tablespoon chopped parsley
1 teaspoon salt
1 teaspoon grated lemon peel
⅛ teaspoon white pepper
1 cup milk
2 pounds perch fillets

Sauté mushrooms and green onions in ¼ cup butter until just tender. Mix together 2 tablespoons butter, parsley, salt, lemon peel, pepper, and milk; heat until boiling. Add perch, cover with sauce and simmer until flesh is just firm. Spoon sauce over serving. Serves 6.

White Perch in Beer Batter

4 tablespoons cooking oil or bacon drippings
6 tablespoons flour
2 tablespoons cornmeal
½ teaspoon chopped dill or tarragon
½ teaspoon salt
1 teaspoon paprika
¼ (12-ounce) can beer (3 ounces)
4 white perch, cleaned
Lemon juice

Heat drippings in a skillet. Mix together flour, cornmeal, dill, salt, and paprika. Add beer and beat until smooth. Sprinkle perch with lemon juice and dip in batter one at a time. Sauté on both sides until flesh is firm. Serves 4.

White Perch Casserole

2 pounds white perch fillets
10 new potatoes, peeled and halved
2 cans condensed cream of celery soup
3 cups milk
¼ cup diced ham
¼ cup diced onion
¼ cup grated mozzarella cheese
6 slices American cheese

Coat a 2-quart casserole dish with vegetable oil; add perch. Place potatoes around edges. Mix together and heat soup, milk, ham, and onions. Pour over fish. Sprinkle with mozzarella cheese and bake 3 hours at 200°. Cover with American cheese slices and warm until melted. Serves 6.

White Perch Fillets on Toast

½ cup flour
Salt and pepper
2 pounds white perch fillets
2 eggs, beaten
1 garlic clove, minced
4 tablespoons butter
6 pieces of bread, toasted

Combine flour, salt, and pepper. Dip perch in egg and dust with seasoned flour. Sauté garlic in butter and then sauté perch on both sides until just brown and firm. Serve on toast. Serves 6.

Hill Country and the Big Red Squirrel

There was a time when the big red squirrel was the king of the hardwood hills. In recent years they have again become more plentiful. As a young child, I wondered why my Dad, when we were hunting, would become so excited when we found an area full of red squirrels. It seems that when he was a youngster he had filled many a family stew pot with them. His Uncle Jake would give him one shotgun shell and what he did or did not get with that one shell was what they ate for dinner. Red squirrels are more plentiful now and are much larger than gray squirrels. It is important that you clean squirrels as soon as possible and allow them to cool. Warm squirrels are the easiest to skin as the skin is fairly easy to pull off and two people make quick work of the job. Young squirrels are always tender and even old squirrels can be mouth-watering good when cooked in a stew or slowly simmered in a skillet.

Spicy Squirrel Mulligan Stew

3 squirrels, quartered
3 onions, chopped
1 green pepper, chopped
2 potatoes, cut into large pieces
4 tablespoons chili pepper (optional)
Salt and pepper
Dash Tabasco sauce
¼ cup chopped celery
1 cup cooked rice

Stew squirrels in a little water until tender. Remove meat from bones. Place meat back into liquid and bring to a boil. Add remaining ingredients except rice and cook 45 minutes or until vegetables are tender. Add rice and serve. Serves 6.

Squirrel Croquettes

2 squirrels
Salt and pepper
Sage
1 egg, beaten
¾ cup milk
2 tablespoons flour
Cornmeal
Butter or oil

Quarter squirrels; simmer in water until meat falls off the bone, remove and let cool. Work meat off bones and chop fine. Season with a little salt, pepper, and sage. Combine egg, milk, and flour; add to meat. Shape into small cakes and roll in cornmeal. Fry in butter or oil until brown. Serves 4.

Squirrel Casserole

5 to 6 squirrels, boiled until tender
1 stick butter, divided
2 cups cornflakes
1 teaspoon garlic powder
1 teaspoon onion powder
1 bag medium egg noodles
1 cup flour
2 cans chicken broth
1 teaspoon salt
½ teaspoon pepper
1 teaspoon thyme
1 cup shredded mozzarella cheese
½ cup Durkee/Frenches fried onions

Boil squirrels and allow to cool. Melt ¼ stick butter in a skillet over medium heat, add cornflakes, garlic and onion powder. Cook briefly until just crisp. Place cornflake mixture into a casserole dish. Boil noodles, drain and set aside. Melt remaining butter in a skillet, add flour and gently brown. Add broth and stir until it thickens. Pull meat off bones, add spices and mix. Cover with cornflakes then cover with shredded cheese and processed onions. Bake at 275° for 45 minutes.

Simmered Squirrel with Rice and Potatoes

Cooking oil or bacon drippings
2 squirrels, cut up
1 onion, chopped
1 green pepper, chopped
¼ cup chopped celery
1 garlic clove, minced
1 cup uncooked rice
3 medium potatoes, diced
Salt and pepper
Water

Heat oil and brown squirrels. Place squirrel in a pressure cooker and cook 15 minutes. Re-heat oil in a skillet and sauté onion, pepper, celery, and garlic until just tender. Add rice, potatoes, squirrel, salt and pepper and enough water to cover. Cover and slowly simmer until tender. Serves 6.

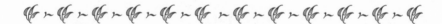

Game Dips for the Super Bowl

Dips and the Super Bowl go together like possum and sweet potatoes. Not many devotees will chance missing a game-changing play by leaving the game to go into the kitchen and wait in line to be served. Not even at half time. Half time is scheduled for bathroom breaks and for reaching into the cooler. Even non-spectators should be spared from cooking during the game. Whether hot or cold, dips can be prepared the day before and will add to the festivities of the day. Finger foods are okay but it is the dips and chips that are always the first to be eaten. Besides being easy to eat, they are quick and easy to prepare, store well, and are inexpensive. Place the dips in smaller containers rather than one large container, place them in the sitting areas, and be prepared to refill them often. Domestic equivalents can be substituted for the wild species in the following recipes.

Layered Catfish Dip

3 cups water
1 pound catfish fillets
12 ounces cream cheese, softened
2 tablespoons mayonnaise
2 tablespoons Worcestershire sauce
1 tablespoon lemon juice
Dash garlic salt
1 medium onion, finely diced
1 (22-ounce) bottle chili sauce
Parsley springs

Bring water to boil in a skillet, add catfish and gently simmer 5 to 7 minutes or until fish is firm. Flake catfish and set aside. Combine cream cheese, mayonnaise, Worcestershire sauce, lemon juice, and garlic salt. Stir in onion. Spread cream cheese mixture on the bottom of a serving bowl, cover with chili sauce and top with the flaked catfish. Garnish with parsley sprigs and serve with crackers.

Venison Dip

1 pound ground venison burger
½ cup chopped onion
1 garlic clove, minced
1 tablespoon vegetable oil
1 cup tomato sauce
¼ cup ketchup
1 teaspoon sugar
¾ teaspoon ground oregano
⅓ cup Parmesan cheese
1 (8-ounce) package cream cheese, softened

Sauté venison, onion, and garlic in oil until just done. Add tomato sauce, ketchup, sugar and oregano. Cover and simmer 10 minutes. Skim off fat, remove from heat, add cheeses and stir until melted. Serve warm with crackers.

Wild Duck Dip

1 duck, cooked
1 (8-ounce) package cream cheese, softened
1 tablespoon mayonnaise
¼ cup chopped onion
1 tablespoon Worcestershire sauce
1 green onion, finely chopped
Tabasco sauce

Remove duck meat from bones, place in processor and pulse 10 times. Add remaining ingredients except Tabasco and process until very smooth. Cover and refrigerate overnight. Sprinkle with chopped onion just prior to serving. Serve with Tabasco sauce and crackers.

Spicy Wild Hog Dip

7 dried hot peppers
2 tablespoons shrimp paste
1¼ cups chopped green onion
2 tablespoons minced garlic
1 teaspoon salt
½ cup ground wild hog meat
1 cup chopped tomato
4 tablespoons bacon drippings
1½ tablespoons sugar
2 tablespoons water

Grind or process until smooth hot peppers, shrimp paste, green onion, garlic, and salt. Mix ground hog meat and tomato into pepper mixture and set aside. Heat drippings in a wok or skillet. Stir in all ingredients and stir/ cook for no more than 10 minutes. Remove from heat. Serve as a dip with crackers or serve with fresh sliced cucumber, carrots, cauliflower, broccoli, or green beans.

Like Chopping Wood;
Good Chili Warms You Twice

My grandfather was a master chili maker. As he used to tell it, he learned the art of making chili while living in San Antonio during World War II. He was too old for the war and being an auto mechanic by trade, the Army Air Force recruited him as a civil servant. He was shipped off to Texas to be trained as an aircraft mechanic. He and six of his fellow workers rented a house, hired a local housekeeper and were thoroughly indoctrinated into TexMex cuisine. Rosa spoke no English and did not know a collard green from a ham hock, but she could make chili from anything. This was fine with them because food ration coupons would only stretch so far. Granddad loved to eat and he also loved to cook. He and Rosa were kindred spirits and he spent more time in the kitchen with Rosa than at the nightly poker table with the boys. When Granddad returned home and my grandmother found out about he and Rosa spending so much time in the kitchen, she didn't speak to him for weeks. That is until he gave her an envelope full of $50 bills he had saved by not playing poker with the boys. My favorite day in all of winter was when Granddad would take me out to split wood. I would carry it in then we would sit by the warm fire as he made chili. It is memories like these that continue to warm me now that he is gone.

Venison Chili

2 pounds ground venison
½ cup ground pork or beef fat
2 cans kidney beans
2 (8-ounce) cans tomato sauce
3 tablespoons chili powder
½ teaspoon each garlic powder and oregano
½ cup dehydrated onions
1 cup water
Red pepper (optional)
Salt
Cooked rice for 2 to 4

In a large pot, sauté venison and fat until just brown. Add beans, tomato sauce, chili powder, garlic powder, orgeno, onions, and water. Simmer 4 hours over low heat, stirring occasionally. Add more water if necessary. Add salt and red pepper to taste. Serve over rice. Serves 2 to 4.

Wild Turkey Chili

3 pounds ground wild turkey
4 tablespoons cooking oil
2 cups chopped celery
4 medium onions, chopped
2 garlic cloves, chopped
½ teaspoon red pepper (optional)
1 teaspoon marjoram
1 teaspoon cumin
2 teaspoons salt
2 (16-ounce) cans diced tomatoes
½ cup chili powder
1 tablespoon paprika
4 cups tomato juice
2 (20-ounce) cans pinto beans, undrained

In a large pot brown turkey in oil. Add next 11 ingredients and simmer over low heat for 60 minutes. Add beans and simmer another 60 minutes. Serves 8 to 10.

Shrimp Chili

1 tablespoon cooking oil
½ cup chopped onion
½ cup chopped green bell pepper
½ cup chopped celery
1 (16-ounce) can stewed tomatoes
1 (8-ounce) can tomato sauce
2 to 3 teaspoons chili powder
¼ teaspoon salt
⅛ teaspoon white pepper
1 pound uncooked, peeled shrimp

Heat oil in a saucepan and cook onion, green pepper, and celery until just clear and soft. Add remaining ingredients except shrimp and bring to a boil. Reduce heat to medium and cook 20 minutes. Add shrimp and cook until just pink. Serves 4 to 6.

Rare Bit or Rabbit

I once spent a whole winter trying to re-create the types of dishes that my early ancestors might have eaten when they were settling into their homesteads. Most of the wild game and fish like bass, bream, deer, quail, squirrel and duck I had eaten. But for some reason rabbit hunting was not one of my early outdoor activities. Finding recipes for rabbit was no problem. But where could I get a rabbit? Mr. Condi Mack Cooper and his son, Rubin David, came to the rescue. One afternoon I was teaching Mr. Cooper how to re-cane the bottom of an old chair and in walks Rubin David with four fresh rabbits. After many questions, it was decided that I would have to be taught how to skin a rabbit and Mrs. Cooper agreed to teach me to cook them. In one lesson, Mrs. Cooper taught me how to fry, braise, and make a truly outstanding rabbit stew. After dinner she packed up the leftover rabbit to go home with me. She also gave directions to Rubin David to carry all of his future rabbits to me.

Curried Rabbit

1 rabbit, 8 pieces
1 stick butter, melted
¼ cup flour plus more for dredging
Salt and pepper
1 onion, chopped
1 tart apple, peeled, seeded and chopped
1 cup chicken broth
2 cups sour cream
1 tablespoon curry powder
2 teaspoons grated orange peel
Cooked rice for 2 to 4

Brush rabbit with melted butter and dredge in flour. Salt and pepper and bake at 300° until tender. Cool and de-bone. Sauté onion and apple in remaining butter. Add ¼ cup flour and stir until smooth. Stir in chicken broth and sour cream until blended. Add curry powder and orange peel; reheat. Serve over rice. Serves 2 to 4.

Rabbit and Deer Sausage

1 pound venison or other sausage links
1 rabbit, 8 pieces
3 garlic cloves, minced
1 medium onion, chopped
2 bell peppers, sliced thin
1 (16-ounce) can plum tomatoes
½ teaspoon red pepper flakes (optional)
2 tablespoons tomato paste
¼ cup dry white wine or water
1 teaspoon each dried basil and dried oregano
Juice of ½ orange and grated peel of 1 orange
½ teaspoon salt
Buttered cooked pasta for 4

Pierce sausages and simmer in a skillet until browned. Remove and slice into 1-inch pieces. Sauté rabbit in sausage fat, remove and set aside. Sauté garlic, onion, and peppers in fat until tender. Return sausage to skillet and add remaining ingredients except pasta. Simmer 10 minutes. Add rabbit and simmer covered 20 to 30 minutes or until rabbit is done. Serve with buttered pasta. Serves 4.

Simply Fried Rabbit

1 rabbit, 8 pieces
Buttermilk
Flour seasoned with salt, pepper, and paprika
Egg/milk wash
Cooking oil

Soak rabbit in buttermilk overnight. Roll rabbit in seasoned flour and then dip in egg mixture. Refrigerate 30 minutes. Fry in oil until done and golden. Serves 2 to 4.

Canned Rabbit Stew

15 pounds peeled new potatoes
1 stalk celery, chopped
2 pounds onions, chopped
12 chicken bullion cubes
2 quarts (8 cups) canned peas
25 (1-quart) scalded canning jars, rings, and new lids
5 rabbits, cooked and de-boned
Salt

Boil vegetables and bullion cubes in water until vegetables are just soft. Fill scalded jars to ½-inch of top with rabbit and vegetables; add 1 teaspoon salt to each jar and process 3 hours in a boiling water bath or in a pressure cooker 90 minutes. Makes 25 quarts.

Yankee Shrimp

I love lobster. Lobster has to be one of my favorite forms of conspicuous consumption. But the price will cool your heels. At least once a year I must slake my thirst for lobster and make a trip to the fish market. This year it will be to the frozen-food section for either a package of frozen lobster meat or two lobster tails, since it is just Anne and I. Our Scottish heritage will allow me to splurge only once a year on lobster. When I was in elementary school, I was infected with my love of lobster by my dad who once carried me along on a business trip to Providence, Rhode Island. I saw lobster on the hotel menu then asked Dad what it was and if I could order some. As usual, Dad told me I could order what I wished. The waiter served me with a whole lobster that had more red shell than I had ever seen in my whole little life of eating boiled shrimp. The waiter suspected that I might need a little help so he sat down beside me and proceeded to instruct me in the proper way to eat that monster. For years, all I remembered about that dinner was the little bowl of warm lemon water that the waiter sat before me after dinner without telling me what it was for. It smelled good, it looked like soup, and for a moment I considered sipping from it until dad came to the rescue, dipped his fingers into it, and suggested that I do likewise.

Lobster Stew

4 lobster tails
4 tablespoons butter
1 pint heavy cream
1 quart whole milk
1 cup white wine or water
Salt and white pepper

Steam or boil lobster, and set aside to cool. Pick-out meat and cut to ½-inch pieces. Sauté in butter until just firm. Scrape bottom and pour into a large pot. Add cream, milk, and wine; simmer uncovered over low heat 2 hours. Refrigerate overnight. Warm, and salt and pepper to taste.

Lobster Alfredo

2 teaspoons chopped garlic
4 tablespoons real butter, divided
¼ cup white wine or white grape juice
¼ cup clam juice
12 ounces cooked lobster meat
4 to 6 cups heavy cream
½ cup Parmesan cheese
Salt and white pepper
1 pound pasta, cooked
Chopped parsley for garnish

In a medium skillet, sauté garlic in 3 tablespoons butter until just beginning to brown. Add wine and clam juice; bring to a boil. Reduce heat, add lobster, and simmer 10 minutes. Add cream and remaining 1 tablespoon butter; simmer until butter melts and sauce begins to thicken. Add cheese and salt and pepper to taste. Serve at once over pasta and sprinkled with parsley. Serves 4 to 6.

Lobster Cocktail

¼ cup cooked lobster meat
2 tablespoons ketchup
2 tablespoons sherry (optional)
1 tablespoon lemon juice
4 drops Worcestershire sauce
Salt and white pepper
Chopped chives for garnish

Mix all ingredients, except chives, well and chill 1 hour. Serve in cocktail glass lined with a lettuce leaf; sprinkle with chives. Serves 1.

Deviled Lobster

18 large eggs, hard-boiled, sliced in half with yolks removed
1¼ pounds cooked lobster meat
¼ teaspoon minced garlic
½ tablespoon prepared horseradish
½ tablespoon prepared brown mustard
½ tablespoon lemon juice
1 teaspoon dill weed
¼ teaspoon Tabasco sauce (optional)
¾ cup mayonnaise
White pepper to taste
Slivered black olives

Reserve 14 egg yolks. Cut lobster to ½-inch chunks. Mix together all ingredients, except pepper and olives, and process until smooth. Fill egg halves and sprinkle with white pepper and slivered black olives. Refrigerate 1 hour.

Crappie: Not Just a Bigger Bream

Crappie are not just bigger bream. Since they are larger than a big bream and smaller than a bass, you can have the best of both worlds. They are small enough to fry in a skillet and are large enough to get a reasonable fillet. If you are brave enough to venture out onto our reservoirs during February you are almost guaranteed to bring home a stringer that will keep you busy longer than you wish. As versatile as they are, we don't hear much about crappie recipes. I suppose that is because they are so versatile and favorite bream and bass recipes are just portioned up or down. I enjoy crappie because they have much of the same sweet taste as bream and the firmer flesh of bass. Each February my neighbor always brings me his crappie; it is not uncommon for me to be blessed with over 100 crappie in a two-week period. I freeze four fillets per zip-lock bag and cover them with water before freezing. More fish than four fillets per bag are too many for Miss Anne and me. If I need more fish, I thaw more bags.

Crappie Gumbo

¼ cup butter
½ cup chopped onion
1 green pepper, chopped
½ cup chopped celery
1 (28-ounce) can tomatoes
1 can chopped okra
1 cup water
¼ teaspoon dried thyme leaves
Salt and pepper
⅓ teaspoon crushed red pepper (optional)
1 pound cooked crappie fillets, cut small
4 cups cooked rice

Melt butter in a saucepan. Add onion, green pepper, and celery. Sauté until just tender. Add remaining ingredients except crappie and cooked rice; simmer 15 minutes. Add crappie and cook another 10 minutes or until flesh is firm. Place rice in bowls and pour over with gumbo. Serves 2 to 4.

Sweet Fried Crappie

10 crappie fillets
1 (16-ounce) bottle ginger ale
1 cup crushed cornflakes
½ cup crushed Captain Crunch cereal
3 tablespoons flour
½ teaspoon ground cloves
2 tablespoons oregano
1 egg, beaten
Cooking oil
Tartar sauce

Place crappie and ginger ale in a zip-lock bag and refrigerate 4 hours. Combine both cereals, flour, cloves, and oregano. Fill a frying pan with ½-inch oil and heat. Dip fillets in egg, roll in cereal, and fry until golden brown. Drain and serve with tartar sauce. Serves 4 to 5.

Baked Mushroom and Cheese Crappie

1 pound (6 to 8) crappie fillets
Salt and pepper
1 can cream of mushroom soup
1 cup shredded Cheddar cheese
Paprika
Cooked rice or noodles

Spray a baking dish with nonstick spray, season fillets with salt and pepper and lay in baking dish. Pour soup over fillets, top with cheese and a sprinkle of paprika. Bake at 350° 20 to 25 minutes or until flesh is firm. Serve over noodles or rice. Serves 4.

Index

W

Game for All Seasons
Cookbook
makes a great gift.

Your friends and family are sure to enjoy the 292 recipes for 33 varieties of game that are found within this outstanding cookbook which is available in your local gift shop or bookstore.

If not available locally, use the order from on the next page, or call us toll-free **866.625.9241** or visit us on the web at **www.greatamericanpublishers.com.**

Also available from Great American Publishers:

900 recipes make up this outstanding collection created with the everyday cook in mind. Each cookbook features 150 easy-to-prepare recipes using common ingredients that are easily found in your local grocery store (most will already be in your kitchen!).

Quick Crockery Cooking • $12.95 • 160 pages • 7 x 7.5 • You'll be in and out of the kitchen fast with creative crockery recipes that are easy, economical and DELICIOUS.

Quick Desserts• $12.95 • 160 pages • 7 x 7.5 • Get out of the kitchen and   into the fun with more than 150 recipes for the best-tasting desserts of all time.

Quick Lunches & Brunches • $12.95 • 160 pages • 7 x 7.5 • From Shrimp Scampi Kabobs to Caramel Muffins, impress friends and family with a delicious brunch made from 150 quick and easy recipes.

Quick Hors d'oeuvres • $12.95 • 160 pages • 7 x 7.5 • Entertaining friends and family is a snap with quick and easy recipes for all-time favorite hors d'oeuvres and beverages.

Quick Mexican Cooking• $12.95 • 160 pages • 7 x 7.50 • More than 150 quick and easy recipes for meal after meal of pure Mexican pleasure.

Quick Soups 'n Salads • $12.95 • 160 pages • 7 x 7.5 •Preparing delicious, nutritious soups and salads has never been easier.

State Hometown Cookbook Series

Tennessee Hometown Cookbook dishes up a double-helping of local, tried and true recipes and fun-filled facts about hometowns all-over the state.

Lisa Flynt and Kent Whitaker bring you more than 300 favorite recipes that are easy-to-follow and use ingredients that you probably already have in your kitchen. From *Beale Street Barbecue Pork Spareribs* to *Chattanooga Fudge Cake, Grandma's Onion Soup Meatloaf* to *Hunka Burning Love Peanut Butter Pie, Crockpot Brunswick Stew* to *White Hot Fish,* there are delicious, hometown recipes to please everyone.

You'll also enjoy interesting food facts and stories about fun food festivals around the state such as Greater Five Point's Tomato Art Festival whose motto is "The Tomato... a uniter, not a divider — bringing together fruits and vegetables."

Tennessee brings to mind music and mountains, history and heritage, and good food – get a taste of it all in *Tennessee Hometown Cookbook.*

Tennessee Hometown Cookbook • $16.95 • 256 pages • 8 x 9

Coming Soon...

Alaksa Hometown Cookbook
Texas Hometown Cookbook

Call toll-free 1.866.625.9241 for more information or to place an order

---